rob 37 heroin

# rob 37 heroin

robert j. kubiak jr.

# CONTENTS

Paperback ISBN: 979-8-9861112-0-9
Digital ISBN: 979-8-9861112-1-6

# Acknowledgments

There are far too many people to thank, but probably most of all are the fine folks at Blue Cross Blue Shield and covering the dozens of rehabs, detoxes, psych ward visits, and hospitalizations through the years. I also can't forget about all of the counselors, social workers, doctors, nurses, and everybody else who tried to help me help myself despite clearly not being ready most of the time. Your efforts and empathy are not forgotten.

For the paramedics and anyone else who revived me and kept me alive long enough to put this thing together. To the fellow clients and patients I've spent many nights with in various facilities. You're my peeps and you've been through it, and I just want anyone out there still struggling or family members of those struggling to know that there is hope.

Got to thank my family for intermittent tough love and for not completely turning their backs on me and for keeping me in their lives even when I was trying to end my own.

To the plethora of facilities and rehab centers I frequented through the years, and a special nod has to go out to Banyan Treatment Center in Naperville. The last treatment center I attended and the one that worked, right? You created an ecosystem and continue to provide the environment, community, alumni support, and a host of other things far above and beyond what this chronic addict could ever have asked for. The staff at housing and clinical remain an incredibly integral part of my recovery journey. And I suppose I should include a quick thanks to Heidi for administering the booty juice (aka Vivitrol) to me each month and dealing with my ass (literally and figuratively) for almost four years.

To everyone at a meeting that has seen me scribbling every day in my little notebook asking me what I was writing and asking about the book – well, it's finally here, and thank you all for holding me accountable.

As much as I'd love to acknowledge all the meetings and clubs I've been to, the WSAC in Westmont in the first year and since then the WSFC in Naperville has become my second home. Everybody who has sat 'round the rooms with me and shared their story, whether it was in a meeting or outside over a smoke or a vape. I learn from every one of you and sincerely hope you keep coming back.

There are too many people to name everyone specifically, and I don't want to forget anyone, but there's a special place in my heart for my 5 pm weekday peeps along with my 5 am weekend crew at the WSFC. Whether or not you know it, the community and void that I had for so long been seeking to fill is now whole. The connectedness and love I feel every time I'm there is unparalleled and you make it all worthwhile.

To the 516 Light Foundation and everything that Brad and Jess do for the recovery community in the area along with Lauren, Deb, and everyone at Path to Recovery Foundation and all the support they provide and for affording me an opportunity to give back.

To Neil, whether or not he knows it, for convincing me that this whole book thing was even possible and sharing details of his own book projects and tips for an aspiring writer as this thing was just getting off the ground.

For Ernest and the good morning text messages you send me every day since the day I left treatment. It might seem like a small thing, but it was encouraging especially in the early days, and I'll never stop trying to shock you with my crazy ass replies.

To Mason and Rex for their valuable insight, advice, and for ensuring this thing would eventually see the light of day leading up to publication.

Dan, Jacob, Jon, Nick, David, Kerry, and everyone else that did time with me at Banyan and are all still clean 4+ years later. It's amazing! And the sugar fiend in me has to give special kudos to Dan for his delicious heroin cakes – they seem to taste better each year!

And last but certainly not least, a very special acknowledgment to Cathy for her amazing content editing and Bianca for steering this project forward when it was at a standstill. "I want pages, send me pages!" You ladies kept me motivated and driving this thing forward at the very end and for being my sounding board in all my neurotic last-minute moments.

1

# Intro

I've spent almost half my life in and out of treatment centers, psych units, rehabs, hospitals, and detox centers. I feel compelled to share some things I've learned throughout the years.

Maybe it's the series of ECTs (electro-convulsive therapy or shock treatments) administered to me a decade ago or perhaps I was born this way, but I've always felt a little off. Like I wasn't built to withstand the mundane day-to-day activities of life. It's like I've always demanded more from life than life had to give. I was always seeking some sort of escape. From what? I'm not sure, but I just always felt like I needed something else. Something more. Something different. Anything but whatever was right in front of me. I've heard addiction described as an inability to live in the moment. And that has characterized most of my life.

They say depression is a response to past loss, and that anxiety is a response to perceived future loss—and that's where I have dwelled most of my waking life. I was either ruminating and beating myself up about something that happened in the past or terrified about

| 4 |

something that might happen in the future. I could never just live in the moment and acknowledge what was going on directly in front of me. In those rare moments when I could acknowledge the present and current state of affairs, I was using illicit substances. The only times I recall having visceral experiences were when I was fucked up.

Don't get me wrong, it wasn't all bad. I have a mental Rolodex of hundreds of thousands of fond memories from my using days. Almost all my favorite memories from my late teens to late thirties revolve around getting or being high. For a very long time, that's all there was for me. I had nothing else; it defined me, and I was perfectly okay with that. I knew I was 100% powerless as soon as I took each drink and drug, and I had no problem admitting that. Before the consequences and lifestyle became overwhelmingly horrific, I used to celebrate it and own it.

It was a love affair with drugs and alcohol that lasted a long time and, like any unhealthy relationship, the romance and allure that initially attracted me to it became replaced with shame, remorse, and regret. It is a relationship that is destined to implode and the only variable in the equation is how many casualties will result. I'm still here—barely—but that's not the case for some of the brightest minds I've known through the years. Those people could not escape the tentacles of circumstance, and they perished along the way, struggling in the grips of addiction and mental anguish. The relationship must end; it's just not something a person can sustain forever. You bottom out eventually and it all falls apart; the only difference in the outcome is whether the wreckage is permanent.

Since I'm still here, I figured I'd compile this collection of miscellaneous stories that I think someone like myself might find interesting and useful, particularly during those tedious and nerve-racking moments of downtime during early recovery when it is SO fucking painful and difficult. So, if you're struggling right now or if you have a family member or friend who's struggling, keep reading.

For every addict, there are times when you feel like you're barely holding on by a thread and everything feels overwhelming. I felt that way every time I staggered back into treatment or detox or a psych ward. It was as though I was chronically in early recovery. And yes, I get it, nobody understands, and you've got such complicated and complex situations going on right now. You're feeling like even if you could somehow convey the pain to others, they wouldn't understand the magnitude of your predicament. We all think our suffering is unique, but as the days crawl by and the mental cloud clears, you can see there is a solution. And once someone shows you the solution, the situation becomes manageable. If you want an epically better life for yourself or someone you love, you just need to be honest and open-minded, and you will see how drastically improved things can be with a little effort, courage, and acceptance.

I'm telling my story so you can see how, eventually, things worked out for me.

# 2

# The Belt

*Riding along the railings of time*
*Radiating glorious susceptibilities*
*Amidst the autumnal bliss.*
*Manifesting fortified complacency*
*And transcribing the inexplicable*
*With harmonious delight.*
*Organically fixated with unmistakable caution*
*On cognitive appetites with relentless potential*
*Yet decidedly overwhelmed by life.*

My first clear memory of childhood was moving from Lockport to Barrington, Illinois when I was five years old. I was completely lost and devastated—my entire world was uprooted, and everything I had known was left behind. My neighborhood, my best friend Ryan, the shrubs in my neighbor's yard where I fell while learning to ride my bike—everything.

I became vaguely optimistic the day we moved in because our new house was situated on a golf course, and I found that fascinating. Then, as my parents were unpacking, out of nowhere, a fucking hot air balloon landed in our yard, and I was completely mesmerized. It was exciting and everyone from the neighborhood came out to greet us and welcome us to the neighborhood. It gave me a glimmer of hope and helped me forget about everything I had left behind and it provided some optimism about starting over in a new town.

We moved in the day before I was to start first grade at Grove Avenue Elementary School. I didn't know anybody and was intimidated about having to meet new kids and make new friends. I suppose the good news was that I met my teacher, Mrs. Hawthorne, the day we moved in. She lived in the cul-de-sac at the end of our subdivision.

The rules were different back then and my parents started me in school at a very young age. I was the youngest one in my grade, and I would be for my entire life. I was absurdly timid, insecure and at first, had an extremely difficult time adjusting and making friends.

I did well in school but felt very distant and miserable and it became quite clear just how introverted I was. I wish I had my first-grade class picture with me right now to show to you. Everybody was smiling, happy, young, and energetic and there was 'ol Bobby Kubiak in the bottom right corner with the most intense frown on his face—you'd swear someone had just taken away my favorite toy or some shit.

Parent-teacher conferences came and went and at some point, Mrs. Hawthorne stopped waving to us when we cruised by in my mom's blue, wood-paneled station wagon (which years later would come to be known as the 'Virgin Destroyer'). She seemed to avoid looking in our direction when we saw her walking her dog through the neighborhood. As we drove past her, my mom would scowl and call her Stone Face Hawthorne. I never understood why. More than two decades later I learned that during one parent-teacher confer-ence, Mrs. Hawthorne told my parents that with over 20 years of teaching experience, it was her professional opinion that I would be a drug addict by the age of 13. My father had to restrain my mother from reaching over and lunging at her. I thought well, shit, that was kind of crazy. The audacity of this bitch! But, then again, to be fair, she was only off by four or five years.

I had a relatively healthy childhood, played a lot of sports as a kid and my father was always my Little League coach. He worked in accounting and my mom was a teacher. I was the oldest of four boys growing up in your average middle, maybe upper-middle-class, family. The four of us were easy to spot and we got to know a lot of people all over town.

After a bit of a rough first-grade experience, I made a lot of friends and on the surface, things appeared just fine. But that wasn't the case. At home, behind closed doors, things were different. My dad drank a lot, not to the point of being an alcoholic, but it was always excessive. When he drank, he was benevolent and fun, and we all loved to be around him. The problem was when he was sober. He was upset, angry, disgruntled, and liable to snap off at any minute. I don't know if it was the stress and pressure of being in his early thirties and having four boys and an entire family to support or what it might have been. I was always uneasy and scared when I heard the garage door open when he got home from work. I'd be like, oh shit, dad's home, I better straighten things up if they were a mess and I better not have gotten in trouble at school or done anything to upset my mom that day.

I'm not exactly sure how or when it started, but if I got in trouble for any reason I would be sent to my room. I had to lie face down and pull my pants down around my ankles and my father would whip me with a leather belt. My brothers got whipped too. That shit fucked me the fuck up. He beat every ounce of self-esteem and confidence I might have had right out of me. I was terrified of the man.

The worst part wasn't even the beatings themselves; it was the fucking anticipation of it coming – it was almost ritualistic. I'd be lying there, face down on my bed, with my pants around my ankles, tearing up – knowing what was coming. You could hear his foot-steps coming up the stairs and he would take off his belt and loop it and fucking snap it hard so that it cracked and to this day that sound fucking gives me the chills and brings back shitty memories.

I always wanted to get it first and get it over with. Lying in bed, hearing my brothers crying and screaming in the other room, and knowing I was next was the worst. I was terrified and confused. It didn't matter how small the infraction, whether you stole a candy bar from the store, hit your brother, or perhaps the pillows on the couch were simply out of place. It seemed like if he was in one of his moods, it didn't matter.

One day my brother Matt got in trouble at school, and I knew he was going to get it and I could hear him getting beat and I felt bad, but also somewhat relieved that I didn't do anything to get into trouble that day. Then my father came into my room and told me to drop my drawers and I asked why.

He said, "Because your brother got in trouble at school."

Dude, I didn't even go to the same school as him at the time. How the fuck was that my fault? I got whipped that day and that truly fucked my head up. I was now getting beaten for shit I didn't even do. I think that's when I realized that regardless of how well I did in school, or how many strikeouts I threw during my Little League game, it was never going to be good enough and he would always conjure up a bullshit reason to whip me. Just to remind me that I never quite measured up.

God only knows how long the beatings would have gone on, but one day my brother locked him out of his room and called the cops. The physical abuse ceased after that, but the emotional abuse continued and seemed to escalate.

To sum up my childhood in one word, I would describe it as 'confusing'.

This went on for years and he slowly beat all the aggression and anger out of me, and I internalized everything. My brothers and I couldn't talk about it or tell anyone. As time went on, the pain and trauma turned itself inward and manifested itself as severe depression. I was left with severe anxiety, depression, and no self-worth or internal validation. I was just completely uncomfortable in my own skin.

Being the oldest, I had no one to lead the way or show me how to do things or tell me what was cool and whatnot. And I had a fuck of a time trying to figure that shit out on my own. Throughout high school I played a lot of sports and lucky for me, my core group of friends did as well. Without them, it would have been easy to fall in with a different crowd and get fucked-up at a much earlier age.

We did typical mid-to-late 90's high school shit, hanging out at Tower Records and Record Breakers. We went to a lot of concerts, saw a lot of indie films, hit up museums, and were into art and photography. And there was the typical high school nonsense—sneaking out at night and meeting up with a group of girls to hang out. It was just innocent fun.

I was still extremely insecure and unsure of myself but was so wrapped up in remaining busy and being around my friends that I never stopped long enough to recognize it or truly establish my own identity.

One day after school, for whatever reason, a few of my friends were fucking around in my brother Matt's room. He was two years younger than me and wasn't home at the time. I came across a small Maglite flashlight and went to turn it on but when I twisted the top, it fell off. He had hollowed it out, put a screen in it, and made it into a little ghetto-ass pipe for smoking weed. I was shocked. I had no idea he was getting high and that was the first time I saw weed or pot-smoking paraphernalia up close. I was intrigued, to say the least.

Soon thereafter he got caught weighing out an ounce on his bed by my mom. That worked out well for me because suddenly I was the "good" son and he continued to get in trouble. Ultimately, I was able to get away with a lot of things, sort of sliding under the radar, and was given more leniency. You'll see just how that turned out as we look at the beginnings of my usage and the catalysts that propelled me into the world of drugs and alcohol.

# 3

# D.A.R.E. & Recreational Reading

*Wincing away from the everyday trivializations of omnipotence*
*Stalking righteousness methodically and gloriously*
*Abstract refutations and auras unrecognized elsewhere*
*Warmth ratios refracted upon the summer solstice*
*Lubricated cognitions and adopted spontaneity*
*Accumulating dormant tomorrows in the clutter of today*
*Recapitulations unrealized by our cognizant allies*
*Tattered rugs, broken English, and metamorphosized literature*
*Sinking ships with false periscopes and leagues revamped*
*Dissipating domestication pursuits and realizing contagious pride*
*Unraveling ornate, columnar hopes with a villain's tendencies*
*Defensive kitchenware manifesting itself through unreal personi-*
*fications*
*Corner store lingo and back-alley chatter,*
*Speakeasies and barkeeps unfathomable,*
*Intoxicated dreams and 80-proof realities,*
*Hip. Urgent. Mediocre.*

When I try to understand how and why I started using drugs, I think back to the D.A.R.E. program in fifth grade. Officer Friendly, or whatever the fuck his name was, came in to teach us about the dangers of drugs and he used the typical scare tactics employed back then. Videos of black guys hopped up on PCP, angel dust, with apparently super-human strength, fighting off six hospital orderlies who were all trying to restrain him. Just crazy, stupid shit, which did little to deter us from wanting to use drugs.

One day he brought in a briefcase with fake samples of various types of drugs. There was a joint, a small straw with a bag of white powder for cocaine, a spoon & needle with a bag of beige powder for heroin, and well you get the point. I was completely fucking mesmerized. I had never seen these things and I hadn't even thought about using drugs, until then. I was thoroughly intrigued and for the first time I had drugs on my mind, and it became a bit of an obsession. After that, drugs were always lingering in the back of my mind and periodically I would daydream about what they did to you and how they might make me feel, but I was only 10 years old at the time, so nothing came of it.

Fast forward to high school and I noticed one of my buddies at school carrying around a book for what seemed like weeks. Periodically I'd see him reading it and eventually I asked, which class is that for? He told me it wasn't for a class; he was just reading it for fun. I was like, what the fuck? Recreational reading bro? Never in my life would I have voluntarily read a book and it wasn't until college that I read an entire book that was required for class. I was tremendous at bullshitting my way through book reports, so this whole concept was new to me.

The book he was reading was On the Road by Jack Kerouac. My buddy told me all about the author's crazy adventures and these bohemians from back in the fifties called beatniks and described their culture. This resonated with me and piqued my curiosity.

A few weeks later after a 311 concert of all things, we ended up back at my buddy Ian's father's place, and someone put on Drugstore Cowboy. I was enthralled by one of the characters, the old junkie priest played by William S. Burroughs. He was one of the bohemians that sort of lingered on the outskirts of the beatnik movement and was also a relatively well-published author.

Within a week I was at the now-defunct, Borders Books & Music, and I found myself purchasing a copy of one of Burroughs first books—Junky. It was my first venture into recreational reading. I was captivated by the junkies and the description of shooting everything from morphine sulfate to Dilaudid to heroin and everything in between. I was also thoroughly drawn in by the whole lifestyle and going "to cop" and waiting for "the man." I finished the book in three days and promised myself that one day I would try heroin. I had this romantic fascination with it from that point forward.

Shortly thereafter I went to the movies and saw Trainspotting as well as Basquiat, and they fueled my burning desire to find out for myself what heroin was all about. I still hadn't tried any drugs or even begun drinking for that matter, but the seed was planted. I say all that to show that I can ultimately trace my drug usage back to the D.A.R.E. program and recreational reading.

At this point, my group of friends began drinking periodically, primarily at weekend parties and whatnot, but for me, I didn't have much initial interest in alcohol. To me, that was so stereotypical and basic and it's what our parents did, and by this point, I had promised myself that I would never be like my father. I believe it was Mark Twain who said, "When I was a boy of 14, my father was so ignorant I could hardly stand to have the old man around. But when I got to be 21, I was astonished at how much the old man had learned in seven years."

I didn't care to drink, so instead, I jumped right in and decided I would take some acid. I procured two hits of acid-coated Smarties from my younger brother's friend and planned to trip that night with my buddy Ian. That night, outside of the Blockbuster Video on Northwest Highway in Barrington, we prepared to set off on our candy-coated hallucinatory voyage and my first foray into drugs.

I fucking loved candy, so after we did a "cheers" with our respective Smarties like a bunch of fucking nerds, we let them dissolve in our mouth as instructed and waited anxiously to see what this was all about. Soon, the entire world started coming to life in a manner I had never seen before. Things appeared much sharper and succinct and they would morph into new things everywhere I looked. I also experienced a comforting warmth radiating throughout my entire body and everything seemed clear to me. There was nothing I didn't understand, and it was as if I was in my own private universe and completely detached from reality. Nothing concerned me and I was no longer timid or unsure of myself. I had no worries. I immediately realized how much I enjoyed this feeling. I felt like I was in a parallel dimension or some shit and that I had gained an entirely new perspective that I couldn't describe to someone who hadn't tripped.

A few weeks later I was introduced to magic mushrooms. Dude, I had never even heard of 'shrooms, let alone seen them. I'm an incredibly picky eater and I won't even eat cheese or fruits or vegetables for the life of me, but within minutes I was forcing down an eighth of shit-tasting caps and stems. I loved it. I had a fucking glorious time and enjoyed it even more than my initial acid adventure. My best friend and I shroomed every weekend for the remainder of our senior year of high school, right up until we left for college.

That year, between trips, I smoked weed and drank a handful of times. I did enjoy getting high and smoking weed, but what I really loved was tripping. As for the drinking, well, I could take it or leave it. That was how things went until I headed off to the University of Wisconsin-Madison for college. Up to that point, I hadn't been caught by my parents or the police, despite a lot of drunk driving and getting fucked up. Back then it still just felt like innocent fun and there were no consequences.

In August 1997, I was 17, a freshman in college, and I just went nuts. I became a pothead seemingly overnight, which was how I met people and made friends. "Hey, what's up? Wanna smoke?" Come to think of it, that's pretty much how I met most of my friends for the next decade or so.

It didn't take long for me to start fuckin' around with prescription pills, snorting Ritalin and Adderall and popping opiates here and there. I was still an insecure boy, scared of the world and I didn't realize that I was using drugs to escape from reality and to create a sense of identity for myself. Not sure why, but I also got really into nitrous. I bought a little "cracker" from some guy at a liquor store after-hours for $8.00 and they sold 24-packs of whip cream chargers at one of the head shops on State Street called Knuckleheads. You could always count on me to have some balloons and nitrous every weekend my freshman year.

I was also binge drinking frequently because it was expected of you. I tried Ecstasy for the first time, too, and the double-stack Mitsubishi I took was fucking phenomenal. I quickly fell in love with it and Ecstasy became quite problematic for me.

During all the chaos and crazy shit that went down my freshman year, one memory that has stuck with me was the events of that Halloween. A few of us decided to shroom and were all tripping balls and eventually made our way back to our dorm (The Towers) to hang out. I don't know exactly why, or what compelled me to do it, but on a small scrap of paper, I wrote 'I don't know me' and handed it to one of my good friends, Jeff. He read it and gave me his patented nod of recognition and I knew he understood. That was a moment of clarity for me and probably the most honest thing I have ever said – and almost 25 years later, to a certain extent, it still rings true. Eventually, I figured out that the emptiness I felt was the reason I got addicted to dope. But that was a long way in the future and many misadventures later.

# 4

# Cocaine

*Orphaned ideas are relentlessly nurtured in the twilight*
*While children dream of places they'll never know*
*And bearded men drink whisky at hours unfamiliar to most.*
*A fleeting glimpse at genius in a back alley*
*Contemplating antiquity in dime-store windows*
*The smell of lost principles inside a courtroom*
*The unstretched yarn of moral fiber is less than a foot-long*
*Learning to sail on a sea of burdens,*
*Yet drowning in inhibitions.*

The summer after my freshman year of college at the University of Wisconsin-Madison, I was back home in Barrington, Illinois. Just working, smoking copious amounts of weed, you know, the usual maintenance we all do while living with our parents to make teenage life tolerable.

A few weeks before school resumed, one of my college buddies from Western Springs, Illinois and I decided to take a road trip down to New Orleans, where a couple of our friends from school (Jeff and Sam) resided. We would also be meeting another college friend (Alice) who was flying in from Boston.

We were out one night in New Orleans, having a blast drinking at some jazz club all night, and eventually, we made our way back to Jeff's place. We were drinking and sitting poolside, and unbeknownst to me, Sam had grabbed a teener (half-eighth) of cocaine while we were out.

I had never done coke before, and I wanted to try every drug. Sam busts out some lines and as soon as I snorted it, I knew that shit was trouble for me.

I remember saying to Alice, "I like this way too much."

Maybe it was the excitement in my eyes or something, but she responded by saying, "Yeah, I'm kind of worried about that."

We carried on with the typical talking a million miles a minute about mind-numbing bullshit and anxiously awaiting the next line. When we finished it all, I incessantly begged and pleaded with Sam to call his guy to get more. I was being totally obnoxious, and it was super out of character for me. It was an early indication of how much of a hold the yayo would come to have over me.

Sam and I were roommates that year and not a month later, two weeks into the school year, we were selling coke. I got a little crazy with it.

One night, a couple of months into the school year, we were drinking and doing coke late into the night. Jeff chopped up some lines and he and Sam told me, "Yo Rob, this is the last one for you tonight – we're worried about you man." Of course, I'm all fuck that, blah, blah, blah, and I ultimately convinced them otherwise. There was zero fucking chance I wasn't going to be doing more. But that shit stuck with me. That was the first time anyone had ever expressed any kind of concern over my drug usage and the first time I noticed that perhaps I was different than everyone else. Once I started, I simply could not stop. I didn't worry about it though; it wasn't interfering with my schoolwork. I never missed any classes and other than losing more money than I made selling coke, because I was doing so much, I had no consequences and nothing bad had ever happened to me, yet.

At the end of the school year rather than head home, I decided to stay up in Madison for the summer and sublet an apartment with a few buddies of mine. I mean, why would I want to go back home to live with my parents for the summer when I could stay up in school and party every day? It was a no-brainer.

When finals were over, a handful of my friends stuck around before returning home for the summer, but most of the students had left, including my cocaine plug.

That left our plans for this weekend a bit uncertain. At around 9:00 p.m. or so several of us were hanging out marinating ideas for what to do that evening and without much hesitation, I was like fuck it, I'm getting an eight ball (1/8 oz of cocaine), but from where?

One of the guys (Johnny) said he could make it happen, but that we'd have to wait until around 2:00 a.m. which was bar time because his connection was at a bar with friends and wasn't gonna leave to serve us. Okay, that was promising, but that was more than four hours from now, so what the fuck were we supposed to do until then? It's like lyrics from that Tom Petty song, The Waiting is the Hardest Part, right?

Someone said they were gonna order pizza, which sounded good, but in my head, I'm like pizza? Fuck that. Not unless they were gonna deliver it with some cocaine man. I couldn't think about anything else and certainly wasn't hungry for a slice.

Now mind you, a couple of the seven or eight peeps I was hanging out with that evening were good friends. A few were acquaintances and/or roommates of friends who I'd see on weekends or at house parties and things like that. And there were two people who I didn't know, a guy and a girl. The guy's name escapes me now, but I remember the girl's name was Erin, and for the life of me I felt like I knew her from somewhere. The whole night I kept trying to place her and figure out where I knew her from.

At one point I even asked her, "Have I met you somewhere before?"
She said, "You look familiar, and like I know you too, but I don't know from where."

Neither of us could figure it out and if I had to guess it might have been at a rave somewhere the year prior.

My colleagues were munching on pizza, but I was getting restless knowing we had at least a few hours before I could get my grubby mitts on some blow.

Erin mentioned that she and the dude she was with had met some guy at a party who sold heroin and that they had his pager number. That piqued my interest. I had never done heroin. They just kind of put it out there and asked if anyone wanted to throw down on some dope. It didn't take much convincing before everyone agreed to fork over ten bucks to give it a try even though none of us had tried heroin. I didn't know it at the time, but Erin and her friend regularly dabbled with it.

They paged him and he called back. He said it would be cool to come through and to page him again once we were nearby. Sweet. Okay, so he's good. It was a little after 10:00 p.m.

"So, what's the plan?" I asked. "Where do we meet this guy?"
"He stays on the West Side of town and there's a Citgo station just across the way where we can meet him," Erin said.
Okay, cool.

They went on, "Problem is, it's like a 15–20-minute drive from here and we don't have a car. Do any of you guys have a car?"

Nobody did. Fuck man, what the fuck?

I was fiending for something now and the switch was flipped; my addict mind had taken over. I couldn't wait another three hours until bar time for the coke. We could get heroin right now and not having a way to get there was killing me. I wasn't going to let that stop us.

I said, "What if I could get a vehicle?"
"Yeah, sweet, you have a car we can use?"

"I think I might, give me like 15, 20 minutes and I'll know for sure."
"Awesome."

I took off and headed back to the Sigma Alpha Epsilon (SAE) fraternity house.

Now, I don't think I've ever revealed this next part to anyone beyond my sponsor and a few folks in various treatment centers. I also want to preface it by mentioning that much like a lot of the stuff I've done in active addiction, I'm not exactly proud of my behavior.

About a month or two earlier, one of my buddies (Graham) asked me to fish something out of his desk drawer, a bag of weed or something, and for whatever reason, I noticed that there was a spare set of keys to his truck lying in the back of the drawer. I thought nothing of it at the time but it's crazy how quickly my brain retrieved the data moments after realizing that it was our way to get heroin.

I knew he wasn't in town and was back home visiting his girlfriend in Minnesota. Somehow, I convinced myself that it was okay for me to "borrow" his car to buy heroin with two strangers I had met that evening. I was that intent on scoring dope. Full disclosure—I had no intention of asking or telling him about the truck, I just needed to get those keys. I knew from previous experience, which I'm not going to get into right now, that you could get into his room by climbing onto the roof through a vacant room in the house and then hop over to a landing outside his room and climb in through the window. I got the keys without a problem but then there was the issue of getting to his truck. There is limited parking in downtown Madison, and it is incredibly expensive to keep your car nearby, so Graham had his truck parked about half an hour away. All of this slowed the process of getting our transportation. I knew all of this, but I was not deterred. I didn't have the slightest bit of hesitation when my little grand theft auto adventure began.

I jogged the entire half-mile, incredibly anxious and excited at the prospect of scoring heroin. Then I drove back to pick up Erin and the guy she was with. I honked a couple of times, and they came down with a cell phone one of the others had lent them. They were both excited and amped up about the successful vehicle procurement.

"How'd you get the truck?"
I kept it simple and just said that a friend of mine let me borrow it.
"Cool."

We headed toward the west side of town and soon we were off-campus and approaching the gas station. Rather than park in the brightly lit-up lot, we parked about 50 yards away in the lot of a hotel next door. It was a bit darker there and it seemed like a better spot to handle a heroin transaction. They paged their guy when we were a few minutes away, but he hadn't responded. They said they knew he stayed just across the street, adjacent to the Citgo.

"Can we just go over there?" I asked.

They said no, not a good idea and they didn't know specifically which house was his, because they were too fucked up to remember. They paged him again. Crickets.

After about 15 minutes of waiting for a call back from this guy, I started to get concerned. They assured me that he'd call back any second. They could tell that I was getting impatient and after about 30 minutes, I got paranoid thinking about a heroin deal going down in this vehicle that I had stolen.

They paged him a few more times as we sat there, and I could tell they were desperate and thirsty to get the dope. It was after 11:30 p.m. and I thought, by the time we get back, we'll be two hours from getting an eight ball of cocaine. So, if this wasn't going to happen, we'd still have that coming our way soon and we could head back. That was no consolation to them. They were intent on doing anything they could to wait on him.

After almost forty minutes, I said, "Look, this dude hasn't replied to any of your pages, I don't think this is happening. We got to go."

They pleaded with me to give him five more minutes.

I'm like fuck man, okay, still sweating the whole grand theft auto factor in the back of my head. I conceded and said, "Okay, look, I'm gonna pull over to the gas station and grab something to drink and after that, we're going back."

I pulled into the gas station, and they asked me to park next to the payphone so they could try paging him from that number and see if he'd pick up.

"Alright cool, but once I get back, we're taking off."
"Okay."

I felt relieved as I walked in to grab a soda knowing the stress from this mission would be over soon. I reached into the cooler to grab a Cherry Coke. Before I could even close the cooler door, I saw all kinds of flashing lights and three cop cars come screaming into the parking lot. Several officers hopped out.

Oh fuck. My life is over. I'm fucked. I'm going to jail, holy shit. Shit, shit, shit, shit, shit. I didn't know exactly what was happening, but it couldn't be good.

I started trembling. My basic motor skills were still somewhat intact, and I staggered up to the register to pay for my drink. Two officers came in. I made sure not to make eye contact.

One of the cops says, "Which way did he go?"
Fuck.
The clerk points to his left and says, "That way!"

I'm waiting to be handcuffed as the cops ran back out. What the fuck? Maybe they didn't connect the dots and know I was with those two?

The clerk told me the charge and I paid for my drink, trying to play it cool.

"What's that all about man?" I asked.

"Some guy filled his tank full of gas, and sped off without paying."

"Oh," I said, thinking, are you fucking kidding me? Three patrol cars responded to some dude that didn't pay for gas? Must be a slow night in Madison to elicit that type of response.

I was still shaken up and nervous as I walked out. What if their attention suddenly turned to the suspicious stolen truck near the payphone? God forbid, what if they ran the plates or asked for my license? I got to the truck without a problem, and we all breathed a sigh of relief.

"Damn," I said. "That sucks that we weren't able to connect with your guy."

"Yeah, that shit was crazy," Erin said.

We rode home in silence.

When we got back on campus, they asked me if I could just drop them off at their place rather than return to the apartment. It was near the lot where I needed to park Graham's truck, so I said, "Sure, no problem."

I didn't understand why they wanted to go home when we were only 90 minutes away from cocaine. But I thought, good, more for us. I dropped them off, returned the truck to the lot, and headed back over to the apartment where everyone was hanging out.

Johnny asked where Erin and the other guy were, and I told them I dropped them off back home.

"Where's the heroin?" he asked.

I explained the craziness that went down and the cops flying in and that the dude never showed up.

"Bullshit," he said. "They got it. There's no way they'd go home instead of coming here to partake in the eight ball. They just went home to shoot up."

"There's no way they met up with that dude," I insisted. "There were three cop cars in the lot, and they didn't have an opportunity."

"Watch," he said. "I bet they got it."
Crazy.

Near 2:00 a.m. Johnny took off to meet his buddy to get the coke. About 20 minutes later, guess who shows up at the apartment. Erin and the other guy and their eyes are pinned out and they're all fucked up. They said they wanted to go home to push off (inject heroin) because they knew we would only want to snort it and didn't want to weird us all out. Johnny had been absolutely right.

I was dumbfounded. "How the fuck did you get it? When the fuck did you get it?"

They said, when I went inside, they spotted him walking over and were able to grab it just before the cops came screaming in.
Holy shit.

When they pulled out the heroin they had saved for us, it was safe to say that they had helped themselves to generous portions and we had next to nothing.

The good news was that just as we were getting ready to do it, Johnny returned with the blow and we ended up just mixing it all and doing speedballs (a combination of heroin and cocaine, the same combo that killed John Belushi).

The amount of heroin was so minimal that I don't know if it did anything to us. We just proceeded to get all geeked out on cocaine.

So, the moral of the story is don't break into your friend's apartment, steal their car, go with two strangers to buy heroin from shady dudes on the west side of town simply because you're too impatient to wait a few hours for cocaine. Wait, that's a bad moral for a story. It's about having patience. No, wait. It's about patience, not committing breaking and entering, grand theft auto, and possession of narcotics, right? Come to think of it, there is no moral to the story here, just some dumb shit I did one time while waiting for cocaine. It was, however, probably the first indication of the incredibly great lengths I was willing to go to and the risks I was willing to take to get my drugs. And for the record, Graham, if you're reading this, I am truly sorry about "borrowing" the Chevy.

-

# 5

# Company Party 2015

*Subdued mornings amidst the backdrop of rainy, institutional-*
*ized weekdays*
*Cathartic romances forfeited for chaotic possibilities and plausible*
*potentials*
*Time staggers by until a photographic collapse*
*Jonesin' for some caffeine and nicotine to start the day*
*Options unrealized and nervous enthusiasm mistaken for*
*anxieties*
*Uneasiness runs rampant amidst this drowsy awakening hour*
*Quiet solitude for those early risers, but a sense of nausea perme-*
*ates these parameters*
*Flushed forevers down drains of soap-filled sobriety*
*Frustrated tenants fight back the lethargy that becomes so com-*
*monplace*
*Dehydrated dreams and medicated methodologies encapsulate*
*these stoic souls*
*Financing futures with prescriptions alluding to a mystical &*
*questionable recovery*
*Fervent, fleeting, and quasi-fictitious sorrows of the less fortunate*

*Anxious to populate some sort of liveliness within this down-
trodden dayroom*
*Brushing away the emptiness that flows so thick within these
confined walls*
*Clutching onto apparitional realities 'cuz that's all that is left for
these lost soldiers of time*
*Struggling within the padded confines of our subconscious*
*Proud purveyors of creative impulses that linger somewhere be-
tween sanity and insanity*
*Conjuring up medicinal allies and befriending them quite
passionately and regularly*
*For perhaps that's all some of us currently have left*
*Organically inclined fascinations grow increasingly thin*
*Homogenized hope...*

In December 2015, I was working for a company in the River North neighborhood of Chicago. During the 15 years between college and 2015, a lot of shit went down. I was in and out of rehab and got caught up in some really stupid shit. I'm not going to get into it in this book but, if there's interest, I'll include it in future volumes of my story.

Anyway, on December 4, 2015, my company was having a conference and every client-facing employee from all of our office locations, including our new Detroit office, were coming into town. Everyone working for the company, along with their spouses/boy-friends/girlfriends, would be attending. They expected to have around 200 people in attendance. The company rented a vacant bar below our office that was up for sale. They had catering, a DJ, and the leadership team was going to bartend.

A couple of months earlier I wrapped up another round of rehab and everyone from my office knew that I wouldn't be partaking in the partying portion of the evening's festivities. They were watching me like a hawk to make sure I wasn't drinking or anything.

As it happened, though, this huge company fiesta landed on my birthday, and I was celebrating 90 days sober. I wasn't attending Alcoholics Anonymous (AA) or Narcotics Anonymous (NA) meetings or doing a damn thing for my recovery, but I was keeping track of my clean time.

The sales summit ended around 4:00 p.m. and it had been a long day for me and my colleagues. Everyone was ready to get their drink on. The drinking started upstairs in the office before the official party began and I had no problem watching everyone get drunk. I didn't want to be there, but it was expected, and my colleagues wanted me to stay and hang out.

Eventually, we migrated downstairs, and they had a nice spread of food and hors d'oeuvres. Folks from the other locations started arriving and things got rolling. I hung around with one of my coworkers who also dabbled in illicit hard drugs, however, his drug of choice veered more toward methamphetamines. He was doing pretty well at the time, laying off the craziness and he was someone I could kick it with.

After a couple of hours of enduring the party, we went out to have a smoke. I decided I was done with the whole sobriety thing. I mean, it was my fucking birthday. I'd been clean for 90 days. Everyone else was partying and I wanted to get some heroin. I couldn't wait too long because I might not be able to get in touch with my guy Sam.

Normally, when I worked at our River North office, I would take the train downtown, but because I was tasked with bringing a box of plaques and awards to the event, I had my car. It was a perfect storm, and all the pieces were lining up for me to get high again and I felt fully justified in treating myself to a birthday high.

I told my buddy, "Bro, I'm gonna get out of here and go meet my guy."

"I wanna come man," he said. "I wanna try heroin, I've never done it before."

"Dude, if we both leave together, they will know what's up and we'll both be fucked. I can get it for you anytime you like, but I don't know about now bro."

He kind of chuckled, "Yeah, for sure man."

"Alright, well I'm out man, just tell them I took off and went home if anyone asks."

"Cool."

I hustled over to my car, confirmed Sam was good to go, bent the corner, and grabbed a couple hundred out of the ATM at the Chase bank on Grand & Franklin. I made my way over to the Near West Side where he told me to meet up with him. I zipped through the city, amped and ready to toot a bag, but what I really wanted was to shoot up.

As I made my way to meet Sam, I pinged my running mate Justin to see if he was able to hang out. He was living with his girlfriend, Ash, and her daughter in Arlington Heights, and she knows what happens when he and I get together. When I call, I always ask, "Is Ash around, or can you kick it for a while?"

This night he got right back to me and said she was working until midnight and that I should swing through after I get up with Sam.

Sweet.

I got the dope and tooted a bag on my way out to the suburbs. Oh, the sweet relief in tooting that first bag. Having been clean for 90 days it hit me hard and I did another one before arriving at Justin's.

I got to Justin's and he flipped over the couch and started fishing around in the torn underside.

"Bro, what the fuck are you doing?" I asked.
"I need to hide my rigs (needles) here otherwise she might find 'em and I don't need that shit."

Whatever, I'm just glad he had the "works." I hated buying needles from the pharmacy. It made me feel like a junkie and I only subjected myself to it a handful of times. I always felt the need to make up some story or pretend I was on the phone with my grandma who, "needed them for her diabetes." At that hour, even if you do find a 24-hour Walgreens that's open, there is nothing worse than buying nothing but a 10-pack of hypodermic needles.

Having already snorted a couple of bags, the shot put me over the top. My knees wobbled when I pushed off. We were both good and high. I did another one about an hour later. I didn't need it and Justin suggested I not do it. But I'm like, "It's my birthday man."

Not long after that, Justin said, "Ash is gonna be home in like a half-hour man."

"Okay, I'll get going man," I mumbled.

"Bro, you should not drive right now."

"Well dude, I'm fine, plus I need to get out of here before she gets back or we're both fucked."

"True. But bro be careful man you are fucked up right now."

"Yeah, for sure, just gonna go straight home."

I don't remember leaving his apartment, but I felt lost once I got on the expressway. Maybe I went the wrong way or missed an exit somewhere. I wasn't sure if I was heading in the right direction. I nodded out behind the wheel and when I looked up, I was less than two feet behind a semi and flying down the highway. My foot hit the accelerator and I rear-ended it going over 90 mph. The next thing I knew, I was getting hit in the face by an airbag. I slowed down and tried to get over to the side of the road. I realized the guy in the semi isn't stopping.

Holy shit. Holy shit.

He probably didn't realize what happened and kept going. Thank God too, because I would have been in a much bigger world of shit if he'd stopped.

I was shaken up and dazed, probably had a concussion, and maybe broken ribs, I didn't know. I could barely maneuver the car over to the side of the highway. What I did know is that I needed to hide my dope, so I shoved it all in my sock.

My car is fucking totaled. I accordian'd it when I hit this guy with the accelerator to the floor. I felt around, fishing for my phone, but I couldn't find it. I don't know if I passed out from the concussion or how long I sat on the edge of the road—it may have been a moment or two or it may have been 20 minutes.

The next thing I know is I've got a cop knocking on my window. He yanked the door open because it was wedged from the impact of the collision. I immediately vomited all over the ground beside the car. Not a good way to start this exchange.

He's got to be thinking, "Oh this drunk fuck, straight DUI."

He took me to the back of the car and asked, "How much have you had to drink sir?"
"Nothing," I said.

He didn't believe me, so he had me go through the field sobriety stuff and I handled most of it no sweat. He leaned in to see if I reeked of alcohol and he had nothing. I hadn't drunk anything, so I was feeling confident that I wouldn't get a DUI.

Then he flashed his light in my eyes, and I can only imagine how pinned out my pupils must have been.

"What's wrong with your eyes? Have you been smoking any weed?" he asked.

"Dude, I just got hit in the face with a freakin' airbag and I'm probably still dazed from that," I said.

He looked confused.

I claimed, "I must have just fallen asleep and I'm exhausted."

At some point, a flatbed tow truck showed up and the cop allowed me to go back to my vehicle to collect my things. I threw everything in my backpack, and the tow truck driver helped me try to find my cell phone. During the accident, it must have flown under one of the seats. To this day, atop all my other contacts is a contact that he must have entered himself. It's starred, and it's marked as a favorite. The contact's name is "Bert's towing, my car is here from accident." Later, I figured out from his area code that I was somewhere near the Indiana-Illinois border.

The cop returned and told me he was going to call an ambulance while the tow guy handled the car.

"I don't need an ambulance. I'm fine."

"No son, you should get checked out at the hospital you may have had a concussion and we should get you an ambulance."

"No, I'm fine."

"Are you sure?"

Fuck yeah, I was sure. If I went to the hospital someone might find the 10+ bags of heroin I had shoved in my sock. That meant arrest time. That was not an option.

"Well, I can't force you to go but you also can't just stay here on the highway."

The tow truck driver graciously offered to give me a lift to the gas station across the expressway as he headed out with my car.

I couldn't believe I had walked away from the accident, potential arrests, DUIs, lawsuits, etc. completely unscathed. Physically I was banged up, but it could have been way worse.

So, this guy drops me off at the gas station and all I had was my work backpack, my laptop, and miscellaneous stuff I grabbed out of the car before they towed it. It was probably 2:00 a.m. and I didn't know what to do. It was December in Chicago and freezing cold. I had left the work event and wasn't dressed for the weather. I went inside the station to get warm and found a small table with a couple of chairs in the back by the ATM. It was tucked around the corner from the front register and out of sight. I bought something to drink and posted up at the table.

I felt sick and threw up in the garbage can next to the ATM where people tossed their receipts. I did that several times during the next few hours, periodically nodding off and having an occasional smoke. I was still so out of it and high that it didn't even occur to me to snort more dope. I must have been really out of it because normally after crazy shit went down, the first thing I wanted to do was snort a bag.

Eventually, morning approached, and I realized I had to figure something out. I didn't know where I was other than somewhere just over the Indiana border. I felt guilty having spent the night in the gas station, so I bought a couple more drinks from the guy at the counter and said, "Yeah, I totaled my car last night and the tow truck guy dropped me off here. I've got to get back to Chicago, any idea how I might be able to do that from here?"

I was not expecting to hear much more than, "Call a cab or an Uber." But instead, he pointed directly across the expressway and said, "There's a bus depot right there and they have buses running to O'Hare Airport and Chicago every hour or so."

"No way."
"Yessir."

I couldn't fucking believe it. It was only like 150 yards from where I was standing. Crazy. But how the fuck was I going to get there? It was across eight lanes of expressway. I did what any addict would do and fucking decided to cross the expressway. I sprinted across the first four lanes when traffic slowed down, climbed over the median, and did the same thing across the next four lanes. On the other side, I walked through the grass and up the frontage road to the bus stop. I asked when the next bus to Chicago would be departing and luckily there was one within 30 minutes. Perfect.

The bus arrived and several people boarded. I found a seat and figured I would take it into Chicago and eventually make my way to Union Station and catch the Metra back to Western Springs. As I was planning this all out in my head, the guy in the seat next to me said, "Hey man, this might sound weird, but can I give you my phone to take a quick picture of me on the bus for my girlfriend?"

The dude was around my age and dressed head to toe in Chicago Bears gear. He was wearing a Bears hat, hoodie, and even sweatpants. I was thinking, "Shit, fuckin' superfan or something?"

I took a quick pic for him, and we got to talking. He told me he was from around here but was living in California with his girl and was in town for his father's funeral.

"Sorry man."
"Yeah, thanks man."

Turned out, he was on his way to O'Hare to head home. "Where are you coming from?" he asked.

"Well, I got into a car accident last night and totaled my shit, so I'm just trying to get back to Chicago and eventually get home."

"Were you drinking?"
"No."
"What happened?"

"I was just exhausted and kind of nodded out for a sec and rear-ended a semi, but he didn't stop. Lucky for me so yeah, that's what's up."

"Oh shit, were you smoking weed?"

I kind of chuckled. "No, man." I don't know if I sensed something about him or what, but continued, "Full disclosure, I'm a dope fiend, man, but I'm kind of working on staying clean and stuff."

"Holy shit man, ME TOO. Haven't been using for a while," he said.

"Oh, for real?"

"Yeah, just been keeping it clean."
"No way?"

"Yeah man."
"Yeah, fuller disclosure," I said grinning at him. "I'm not doing a very good job with that."

He smiled, "Me neither."
"Dude I've got like some on me now man."

"So do I man. Let's trade. I got Xanax too, you want some Xanax?"
"Um, yes."

We swapped a couple of bags of dope, and he ran back into the bus depot to shoot up and damn near missed the bus. I had just gotten high, so I just hung onto his shit. We chatted it up the entire 45-minute ride to O'Hare. He got off to catch his flight and I hopped off to grab a smoke.

It's crazy how shit like that goes down. It's like addicts have this sixth sense and you can put us anywhere and we'll find whatever we need and identify who it is we need to get it from. His name was Angelo, and we knew each other for maybe an hour, but I'll never forget that day. Before we parted ways, we had someone snap a few pics of us fucking around outside one of the departure gates beside the bus.

It was still early on Saturday morning. The sun was shining, and I had a decent amount of dope. There was no urgency to get home to my father's house and I had no idea what the fuck I was going to say happened with the car. I was just concerned with getting high and staying high in peace all day and I'd worry about the other shit later. I wasn't even thinking about it. That was a mistake. To buy time, I think at one point I shot him a text saying I had crashed at one of my friends' places after the holiday party.

Most of the day was a blur and somehow, I managed to end up near the front courtyard of the Field Museum. I remember nodding out as I was walking past it. I would take a few steps and then stop. Come to. Try to keep walking and then fall out again. It took me half the afternoon to make my way back to the Loop. It was late by the time I finally caught an early evening train back to Western Springs. I hopped off and headed to the Starbucks across the street. I ordered a drink and as soon as they handed it to me, I dropped it.

"Oh my god I'm so sorry," I said.
"No worries, man, it's okay, we'll get you another."

They handed me the second drink and the same thing happened; I dropped it. I must have been nodding out waiting for the second drink. I was a hot mess, and they could tell. They said, "Sir, you have to go. Please go."

I understood and got out of there.

The next several hours are a bit of a haze. The Metra ticketing building was closed, and I must have wandered along the platform.

I remember suddenly realizing that I was incredibly cold and confused. I didn't have a coat, or a hat and it couldn't have been more than 35-40 degrees outside. I felt around in my pockets and didn't know where my phone was. I looked around a bit, but I didn't see it anywhere on the platform. Nobody was around and I remember I kept falling off the platform and onto the train tracks. I couldn't keep my balance and was just beyond fucked up. I ended up with grease imprints of the tracks smeared across my shirt so I must have fallen several times.

The last time I crawled back up onto the platform, I noticed my phone under a trash can. I retrieved it and the screen was smashed to shit and it wouldn't turn on. I didn't know if the battery was dead or if I broke it. I must have dropped it and accidentally kicked it under there at some point.

I was shivering and tried to flag down cars coming down Wolf Road for help. I have no idea what the fuck I intended to say to them or what I would have done if someone had stopped. I even tried flagging down cops that were driving by, but nobody seemed to notice me, or maybe they were uninterested in helping my crazy ass.

I only lived a couple miles from the train station and I could have easily walked home, but somehow that never occurred to me. I don't know, maybe subconsciously, I didn't want to get home and deal with my father.

I nodded off on an outdoor bench and eventually it was morning. I walked into the nearby police station and asked if they could call me a cab or something since my phone was broken and dead.

ROBERT J. KUBIAK JR.

They obliged and I took a cab home as the sun was coming up on Sunday morning.

My father took one look at me, and I can only imagine how flabbergasted he must have been.

First question, "Where's the car?"

"I got in an accident."
"How bad was it?"

"Pretty bad, they had to tow it."
He knew I had relapsed and was high. "Where?"

"I don't know, but the tow truck driver put the number in my phone."
He was ready to start drilling me hard, but I said, "I need to lie down."

I did need to lie down. I was coming off being up all night outside, I probably had a concussion and my whole body ached. I remember lying down and immediately falling asleep. I came to about 24 hours later and sheepishly walked downstairs. My father had spoken to my boss, who was worried about me when I didn't show up at work and didn't call in. My dad had also retrieved my work backpack from the Starbucks where I dropped my drink a couple of times. In all the craziness I had left it behind. I don't know if they gave it to the police or fished through it to find my ID, but amongst a bunch of things my dad had taken care of while I was asleep, getting the backpack was one of them. He had also learned that the car was completely totaled. I'm sure we had a long, arduous kitchen table talk/lecture, but I was in such a daze I don't remember any of it.

The next solid memory I have is seeing how bruised my chest and sides were from all the falls. I also had minor cuts around my neck and face from the impact of the airbag. I suspect I cracked a rib or did some damage to my sternum because for the next two months it hurt to breathe. Laughing was barely tolerable and I couldn't lay on my back. I had to slowly ease onto my side because anytime my ribcage expanded, I had shooting pains and it felt like my chest was about to cave in.

I managed to make it to work on Tuesday and my boss asked me how I was doing. I think he was a bit surprised I wasn't more bruised up from totaling the car, but most of the damage was internal and I had bruises primarily on my torso and arms. I can't remember much else about that period, but I had to take taxi rides to and from the train station each day, take the Metra into Chicago, and walk a mile and a half to get to the office.

The next few weeks and months are a blur of heroin usage. The whole incident didn't slow me down one bit. I stopped going to the aftercare group at the New Day Center in Westmont. I went all-in on the dope usage. Needless to say, my presence is no longer requested or required at our company's holiday parties.

# 6

# Compartment Syndrome

*Drowsy weekdays on overcast shadows of solemn regrets*
*Implausible explanations are exercised to their utmost ability*
*Eyelids weigh a thousand pounds and tangible diagnostics are inexcusable*
*Forfeiting integrity and desire for listless lies and distraught domestications*
*Colossal conditioning and irksome repetitions allude toward tradition*
*Permanence is a forgotten fallacy with no constitution to speak of*
*Reconstructing compensatory rays of brilliant, sunny hope*
*Clutching onto calibrated visions of ultraviolet hues in every imaginable color*
*Damp, wooded confines that quietly trickle the humid drips of rainwater*
*Amongst the rain-soaked parables that explain this entire predicament*
*A young child quietly swings on a bench on the porch of her ranch-style home*

*Humming historically Christian hymns and waiting for the rain*
*to cease*
*For as the garden grows, so does the impatience of lost innocence*
*Corrupted definitions and stunning implications abound*
*The restoration situation has become somewhat ominous*
*Thwarting knowledge and freebasing exotic vernaculars*
*Sun glistens through the tree branches and creates a hazy reality*
*Your sensitivities are heightened and a cool, damp musky scent*
*permeates*
*A sticky feeling of clammy corridors blankets this grassy knoll*
*Timeless treasures of rural acquiescence – forever – tomorrow.*

Twenty sixteen was not a productive work year for me given the level to which my heroin usage had escalated. I was copping during work and cooking up shots in the office before my coworkers arrived. I nodded out at my desk and was dope sick all the time because I was too broke to buy more. My boss and others tried to help, and they even organized an intervention with me one day after work. One of my boss's buddies who had been sober for a few years tried talking to me. Nothing worked.

One morning I was in the small conference room with my boss, and he told me that I had called in sick 68 days since the beginning of the year. I knew it—my time at the company was about to end. I was done. He had a whole diatribe prepared, and it ended with, "The only reason I'm not firing you is that I am certain that if I do you will die within 60 days."

He was right. It probably wouldn't have taken that long. I was so grateful. At that point, aside from identifying as a semi-functioning junkie, my entire identity was tied to work and my professional life. I was living a high-risk, high-reward lifestyle and when things were good, they were great, but when things were bad, they were incredibly bad.

I started attending the lunchtime AA meetings that my boss's friend had suggested. I walked to the meeting every day from our office in River North. That lasted for a while, and I laid off the dope for a few weeks. But it wasn't long before I was copping after the meetings on my way back to the office. I slowed down a bit, but things were beginning to get bad again.

Right after my birthday in early December, I orchestrated grabbing some dope with a couple using buddies of mine (Justin and Jake) who mentioned they had found a new hookup with some fire dope. I was into it, and they picked me up near the Merchandise Mart Friday after work. We headed to the new spot just west of downtown. I didn't know where we were going, but their new hookup was going to meet us at a BP gas station along the 290 expressway near the Independence exit. Ironically, it was a block away from Gateway Treatment Center.

It felt hella shady, but the deal didn't take long, and we were back on 290 in a few minutes. I can't remember whether they dropped me off at my house or if they took me to the Metra station and I took the train home. Perhaps that's some indication of how bad my addiction was getting, and the kind of shape I was in. Either way, I managed to get home, and I distinctly remember the small bags the dope came in. My buddies told me it was super good shit and that I only needed half a bag. I figured it was laced with fentanyl or something.

I grabbed my tools (spoon, cotton, water, needle, lighter) and intended to only dump out half the bag, but I spaced out and dumped it all out. Damn. Whatever. It's Friday night. I didn't have anything to do the following day. Whatever.

The next thing I remember is coming to about 12 hours later. I was lying on the ground next to the sofa in my room, fully clothed with the television and lights still on and my right leg was completely asleep. I couldn't move it. I drifted in and out of consciousness. I remember a vision of the TV in front of me playing static and Jake, one of the guys I was with the evening before, was standing off to the right of the TV. I kept saying his name, "Jake, Jake." It was as if I was calling out to him, trying to get his attention for some reason. Maybe I wanted him to fix the static on the TV, I'm not sure. I sort of woke up again. I was laying in the same spot and my freaking leg was completely numb and I couldn't move it.

An hour passed and I figured my leg would start getting that pins and needles feeling and wake up. But nothing. I still couldn't move it. What the fuck? I leaned over to try to pull myself off the floor and onto the couch and I realized that the black rectangular thing at the end of my laptop's power cord was wedged under my back. I thought that had something to do with cutting off the circulation in my leg or pinching a nerve or something. I slid it out from under me and tried to pull myself up on the couch, but I couldn't even bend my leg. Oh shit. I felt horrible pain when I tried to bend my knee. Something was seriously wrong. Oh shit.

I was still out of it, but the shock of the pain jarred me back into reality. I yelled for my father, "Something is wrong with my leg, and I think I need an ambulance."

The pain was setting in hard.

At first, he was pissed and didn't respond because he knew I was high and fucked up. I kept yelling and when he recognized the situation was severe, he came into my room. I glanced to my right, and we both noticed the uncapped needle lying beside me on the couch. I don't think he had ever seen a needle before, and I don't think he knew that I was shooting up. He suspected I was using heroin, but I think the needle was a bit of a shocker. I mean for any parent, that would have to be quite unnerving.

He called an ambulance, and the paramedics put me on a stretcher to carry me down the stairs because I couldn't walk. I passed out. When I woke up, I was at Loyola Medical Center in an intensive care unit, closely monitored by an attendant. They told me that I had suffered from compartment syndrome. This is a condition that can happen to intravenous drug users who overdose because the blood flowing to a leg does not get recirculated and collects in the lower leg. I don't know if the laptop power cord made it worse, but it happened because I overdosed, and my body didn't move like it does when you go to sleep. I hadn't moved for hours. Had I been wearing shorts when I fell out, I would have seen that my lower leg had ballooned to three times its size and I would have recognized something was wrong a lot quicker and wouldn't have assumed my leg was asleep.

They performed an emergency fasciotomy to try to save my leg and avoid amputation. Now fasciotomy sounds all fancy and complicated, but all they did was cut four 12" incisions, one on each side of my calf and one on each side of my thigh. Yeah, they basically took a blade and just sliced my leg open to relieve the pressure and drain out all sorts of blood and fluid. My entire leg was connected to the equivalent of a colostomy bag while fluid drained out. I could only move my upper body and my left leg, and I couldn't get up or move around. Since I couldn't get up, they hooked me up to a catheter. I didn't know it then, but this situation would last a long time.

They also told me that my kidneys were functioning at three percent of normal. I was rolled down to the dialysis center in my bed a few times a week for the next month. I spent Christmas on dialysis. I was hopped up on heavy doses of morphine to ease the pain. They knew I was a junkie, but this was not a grin-and-bear-it type of situation. I was fucking miserable. They kept telling me that I was lucky they didn't have to amputate and that they were confident that eventually I would get feeling back and hopefully be able to walk again.

I was in a dark place in that hospital, man. I couldn't get up. All the food was incredibly bland because they had me on a renal diet to protect against the kidney issue. I didn't go to the bathroom for three weeks, just had the catheter. They bathed me in my bed and rolled me over onto my side because I couldn't do it myself. It was painful and miserable. All I could do was lie on my back and try to sleep or watch TV. I'm pretty sure I saw every episode of Forensic Files ever created. FYI, it's all about the splatter patterns and the DNA.

Anyway, when they managed to get my kidneys back close to status quo, I was able to piss and shit again, and once the draining of my leg was over, they stapled me up and told me that the next step was to work with a physical therapist. I would have to learn to walk again. What? Are you kidding me? I figured if I just swung my legs over the side of the bed, I would be fine and would be discharged soon. Boy was I wrong.

The atrophy from not moving my leg for a month and the surgery and incisions they made to save the leg meant I had nerve damage and no motor skills. I was in full-on self-pity mode at that point. I told them I didn't care if I could walk again. I wanted to give up. But I couldn't go anywhere or do anything about it, so they forced me to work with the physical therapist (PT). They helped me stand up and sit upright in a chair for 30 minutes a day. My entire body, and especially my leg, throbbed with pain. I was very combative during this whole process.

After a month of this, they told me they were transferring me to another hospital, the Rehabilitation Institute of Chicago, now known as AbilityLab. They said I would continue to work with a physical therapist and relearn how to walk. It sounded miserable. I wished I had died when I overdosed.

At the new hospital I shared a room with another fellow who was also in bad shape. He had his own ailments, and I was a hot mess.

The first step was learning how to stand up on my own, doing stretches in a wheelchair, and other kinds of therapy. Then I had to learn how to slide off my bed and get into the wheelchair myself. They were still "hopeful" I would be able to walk on my own again.

That did not exactly give me confidence. I thought, are you fucking kidding me? I'm doing all this painful shit every day and there's a possibility that I may never be able to regain full feeling in my leg and foot and walking on my own was only a "strong possibility" contingent on working with the PTs?

The next goal was to get from the wheelchair to a walker by myself and eventually to a cane. If all went well, I would be able to lose the cane at some point. I still needed help doing everything. They had to help me into and out of the bathroom. I couldn't even wipe my own ass, so they did it for me. It was a completely ego-deflating process.

Eventually, I had some positive results and after another three or four weeks, I was comfortable navigating around using a walker. They explained that once I left, I would require ongoing intensive physical therapy five days a week. They also said I would need a seat in the shower because although I could stand up and move around with the walker, I had a long way to go before I could stand up for more than a few minutes at a time. I didn't like the sound of it, but after having been in the hospital for going on two months, I wanted to get home. Going home meant that my father had to take care of me. Help me up and down the stairs and take me to physical therapy every day.

The entire time I was in the hospital I remembered the untouched bag of really good heroin that I overdosed on. I kept romanticizing about getting it. A few days after I got home, my father went out for dinner with some of his friends and left me alone for a couple of hours. Now was my chance. I crawled up the stairs and into my room and fished the bag out of its hiding place.

I crawled back downstairs, sweating and exhausted. I dumped out a line and snorted it and I was in heaven. I was already hopped up on prescription opiates for the pain, which my father was keeping out of reach and doling out as prescribed.

You'd think that after all the shit I had just gone through, I'd want to lay off the heroin, but that's the power of addiction. Life seemed okay again when I was high. All I was doing at that point was sleeping on the couch in the living room, so I was confident that my father wouldn't suspect I was high. It was going well but in the middle of the night I had to go to the bathroom. On the way back, I must have grabbed something out of the fridge because I fell in the kitchen and my walker slid out from under me. I tried to pull myself back up and get to it using the counter, but I was so weak I failed. I tried again. I was trying to be quiet because my father was sleeping in the La-Z-Boy chair in the next room, and I didn't want him to find me fucked up.

Just as I got myself back up and my walker upright, I heard, "Rob. Rob, you okay?"
"Yeah, just grabbing something to drink."

He went back to sleep, and I hobbled back over to the couch. Close call. And that was it for the rest of the dope, which sucked because I had no idea when I would ever be able to get more.

After a month or so of physical therapy, I was making a little progress. I met with the doctor, and he said that they would not renew my oxycodone prescription. They weren't going to wean me off it or anything. After three months of daily usage and even stronger stuff, morphine, etc. in the hospital this was gonna be painful. I pleaded with this guy to continue it, trying to appear as non-addict-like as I could, but I kept getting a hard "No." That's when I learned what pain really was.

Every day for the next couple of months, I would be writhing in pain by around 4:00 -5:00 p.m. It didn't matter if I had laid in bed all day or moved around, like clockwork, by the late afternoon my foot was throbbing. Something to do with the nerves regenerating and the damage done by the accident. It was almost intolerable. The pain alone had me longing for heroin just to be able to sleep through the night. I was miserable. I tried everything to make it stop. Cortisone shots directly into my heel, acupuncture, ice, heat, over-the-counter meds, everything. Eventually, 2400mg of Gabapentin along with some other non-narcotic pain medication made it somewhat manageable.

In addition to the arduous PT, I had a morning routine of cleaning and applying new bandages to the large open wound that was still healing on my right leg. I had a wound because there was a place where they couldn't sew up the leg and they had done a graft with skin from my left, upper thigh.

To make things a little more stressful, my employer graciously allowed me to work half days from home after my morning PT. I'd get home from PT, eat something, and then work for 4-5 hours. This started immediately after I was released from the hospital. Granted, I understood the urgency to get me back to work after having been out of commission for over two months. I mean shit, I couldn't believe they stuck with me through this whole debacle. Our CEO had even visited me in the hospital along with one of my coworkers, (Jeff) which was cool.

Ultimately, the pain became somewhat manageable, and I was down to three days a week of physical therapy. At this point, I had "graduated" from my walker to a cane although I had a solid limp and limited mobility in my right foot. I couldn't run or jump or turn it from side to side. They had me work with rubber bands, stretching, and a host of other miscellaneous exercises to hopefully get back to full usage.

As PT was winding down and I was able to get around a bit with my little cane, I made it back to the office. Now, I had ulterior motives for wanting to get back to work. I needed some alone time after having been cooped up in my father's house all that time, of course, and I wanted dope. Literally one day after being back in Chicago, I called my heroin dealer. I met him near Union Station, and he chuckled about the cane situation. I didn't explain the whole story, I just said I jacked up my knee.

Within a week I was a complete and utter mess. I passed out on my laptop at work, sweating profusely. There was no hiding it. They sent me home that Friday and on Sunday I was in Hinsdale Hospital with pneumonia, barely capable of breathing and dope sick. It happened that quick. It was kind of ironic that my life had at this point come full circle. I was being admitted to the same hospital where I was conceived thirty-seven years earlier.

They got me a bed and began nursing me back to health. After a couple of days, good old Dr. Richard Ready paid me a visit. For those of you that have never done treatment at the New Day Center, this guy is a legend in the West Suburban Chicago recovery community. I knew him from my stint at New Day a year or so prior. He gently and kindly patted my leg and said, "Robert, you need to go back to Residential."

Shortly after that, one of the nurses came in with a list of treatment centers and a telephone for me to try to find myself a bed. After my week-long relapse, I had been booted from my father's house. "No longer welcome," I believe were the exact words used.

I was hopeless, dope sick, and heading back to treatment. I could sort of walk, but still had my cane. My continued employment was very iffy at that point.

Fortunately, I managed to secure a bed at Gateway West. They work with a lot of folks that are on Medicaid or who don't have insurance, so once they found out I had BCBS PPO, I was in. They said they would send a driver to pick me up as soon as I was discharged. Cool. Glad that was easy.

The following morning, I gathered up my things and made my way back to the cozy confines of Gateway West. As we exited the expressway and got off 290 and onto Independence, we passed the BP where this whole mess started. Sure as shit there were dudes posted up outside, ready to serve anyone who pulled in looking for blows (i.e., heroin). If I thought being admitted back to Hinsdale Hospital was ironic, driving past the BP was when things really came full circle. Something about the combination of the two gave me a cozy, embryotic, nostalgic feeling of detachment. It was oddly familiar, and I immersed myself in that feeling during intake.

The warm and cozy feeling evaporated when a 6' 5" black former Army veteran named Wade took me into the laundry room and had me strip naked for him. That's when I knew I was back at Gateway Foundation, and it was time to switch back into recovery mode.

# 7

# Orange Fanta & Oyster Crackers

*Apathetic landscapes permeate natural beauty amidst the backdrop of a thousand tomorrows*
*Clouds part and suns set while a deep fog rises from a nearby marsh*
*The lowlands of our perception are nestled neatly beside the glory of the horizon*
*Championing perfection on a tadpole as swans slowly creep by*
*The animalistic instincts in all of us explore this vast, natural playground*
*The spectrum of colors is quite overwhelming and manipulates heightened sensitivities*
*Nurturing thy young and expressing affection as a flute caresses the soundtrack*
*Purity in its most blissful and untainted state – truly remarkable*
*Capturing horizontal colors and shades unknown*
*A lonely fisherman at a secluded pond embraces the unreality of this Earth*

*The brilliance is quite remarkable, and no picture or painting can
capture the essence of life at a moment like this
Every image – a postcard really – a true sign of natural harmony
unbegotten by instincts
Flirting with metaphysical everythings and grasping metaphorical
nothings
Preservation, deliberation, contemplation – it all adds up in
perfect visceral balance
A heavenly motif encompasses us all as we float silently away and
dissipate amongst the clouds.....*

We pulled up to the entrance of Gateway and the place seemed eerily familiar. Once inside, the gentleman doing intake, John something-or-other, also seemed familiar. It hit me that I had been there before. Back in 2009. I was in their dual-diagnosis program which was a co-ed program and separate from the standard male and female units. The last time I was there, it was when Michael Jackson died. I also remember keeping a journal and writing a lot of free verse back then, but the most memorable thing about that first experience was the ridiculously twisted joke my roommate (Luis) told me as we were making our beds one morning.

Kind of out of the blue, he said, "What sound does a baby make in the microwave?"

"I don't know, what?"
"I don't know. I was masturbating too loud to tell."

Holy fuck, I nearly lost my shit and was hysterically laughing. Now to the non-drug addict a statement like that might get you called into HR and terrify everyone within earshot, but in a treatment center basically, anything goes and the more shocking or absurd, the more likely people will laugh at it.

This time I'd be headed to the men's unit, where like a lot of treatment centers, males and females were separated and there were strict "no fraternizing" policies in place. By the time I finished all the paperwork, saw the nurse and they had searched through all my belongings it was late Friday afternoon. I was escorted up to the unit. There was a large common room with a television on both ends and several guys lounging around on couches and chairs. The gentleman asked if any of them were in my assigned room. One of the guys, Mike (deceased April 2020, overdose), popped up and showed me to our room. It had four twin beds and a bathroom. He pointed to the open bed and started going over the run-down of expectations and his take on things. I listened to him as I made my bed and we headed back to the day room for the Friday night movie and pizza, which is something of a Gateway West tradition on the men's unit. With that, I settled back into the rehab routine.

The next morning the entire unit reconvened in the day room for morning check-ins. We took turns around the room and stated our name, age, drug of choice (DOC), and a positive affirmation for the day. When I first arrived, I was kind of timid and long-winded.

"Umm, my name is Rob. I'm uh, 37 years old and my drug of choice is heroin. And an affirmation? One day at a time."

But after a couple of weeks, it was just, "Rob, 37, heroin...." It got to the point where a handful of guys and a few of the staff started

ROBERT J. KUBIAK JR.

referring to me as "Rob 37 heroin" and I just kind of ran with it. That's when the moniker was born.

Unlike some treatment facilities where you needed good insurance to be accepted, Gateway Foundation, while I was there anyway, was a hybrid. Some clients had come right in off the streets without insurance. Some were homeless and some came directly from prison. Others had insurance and others were gainfully employed. It created an interesting and diverse recovery dynamic and provided a wide array of experience, strength, and hope from all walks of life. You never knew what to expect when a new admittance joined the unit.

David, who turned out to be our new roommate, was definitely unexpected. He showed up in a purple, pleather suit with a three-spike 10" mohawk and patent leather shoes. He looked like a garbage pail kid on acid. He was dirty, loud, narcissistic, and certifiably nuts. I loved him immediately. Well, let's not say immediately, there were times he could be so obnoxious that nobody could stand him, but we found a common bond with our respectively, dark, twisted sense of humor.

Our friendship began innocently enough one day in a group activity. We were tasked with writing down three things that we wanted to try when we got sober. So, we're going around the room and the mood is kind of light and optimistic and everyone is listing their three things. It comes around to David and he said, "Skydiving, swimming with the dolphins, and consensual sex."

There were a few snickers and a loud outburst from me. The expression on the counselor's face was priceless. I couldn't stop chuckling to myself about it. Let's just say he had me at "consensual sex." Wait, that just sounded hella weird, but you know what I mean.

One of the most important features to me of any rehab/treatment center/psych ward/detox center/hospital, etc., is the food. In some cases, it is the only thing to look forward to and it can make or break the day. For instance, I will never forget the delicious Oreo pie at Holy Family Keys to Recovery in Des Plaines. Or the incredible brownies that came individually wrapped (supposedly by inmates at Cook County Jail) at Madden Mental Health Center. They were so good that on more than one occasion I've considered having a psychotic episode just to get my paws on another one of those delightful treats. On the flip side, I remember, with startling accuracy, the horrid food served at Choices Recovery in South Bend and how filthy the kitchen was. You would open a cabinet and fruit flies would come buzzing out.

Gateway West was somewhere in between. On some days you'd get decent BBQ chicken, hot dogs, or pizza, but most of the time it was something I wouldn't touch. I found myself filling up my cup with orange Fanta (no ice, always no ice) and grabbing handfuls of oyster crackers before heading down the cafeteria line. More often than not, I ended up with a tray of 5-10 bags of oyster crackers and my orange Fanta and that was it. It became something of a running joke with the other patients. One day it occurred to me as I was scribbling in my journal, that, if I ever wrote a story about my Gateway experience, I'd call it "Orange Fanta & Oyster Crackers." Now I have.

When I arrived at Gateway, I wasn't convinced I wanted to get sober. I was there because I had run out of options. I knew I needed to get clean, I just didn't want to. I had tried the "functional" junkie thing for years and it wasn't working. I had done sobriety. At one point, I had accumulated almost two years sober, but I had been miserable. I hated it. I had been just white-knuckling it most of the time. The first year, I went to a ton of meetings, but I wasn't working a program and eventually I stopped and went back to the dope. This time my plan was to give recovery a try but if I was still miserable at discharge, I would find a cheap hotel room, do a couple jabs (24 bags) of heroin and overdose.

In a small group session one day, I said, "I can do sobriety, but sobriety sucks." One of the other guys, Mike, I believe his name was, told me that I needed to connect and find friends in recovery—people that I could do things with and have fun with. I had heard that hundreds of times before, but my dis-ease makes me terrified to reach out and connect with people. For whatever reason, this time the advice stuck with me. I remembered it later, much later, when I was finally actively working on recovery.

Midway through my stay, a new client, Miguel, joined our unit. He spoke broken English and the language barrier and rehab clearly made him uncomfortable. I wondered whether he understood precisely where he was and if he would get anything out of his stay there. When he finally did speak at morning check-ins, he had a staggered, effeminate, nasal Hispanic accent and said, "Mi nombre es Miguel y tengo problemas con alcohol."

Right as he spit it out, David and I made eye contact and started chuckling. There was just something amusing about how timid he was and his voice and mannerisms. What was probably just an innocuous check-in comment for everyone else, somehow managed to become an evening game for David and me. Lights out was around 10:00 p.m. and we never could get to sleep. In the dark, lying in bed, we'd just talk shit and try to make one another laugh. I can't remember who started it, but we would impersonate Miguel and his whiny Hispanic accent and conjure up fictitious addictions.

"Mi nombre es Miguel y tengo problemas con blotter acid."

"Mi nombre es Miguel y tengo problemas con Dr. McGillicuddy's."

"Mi nombre es Miguel y tengo problemas con mescaline."

"Mi nombre es Miguel y tengo problemas con Tito's handmade vodka."

"Mi nombre es Miguel y tengo problemas con morning glory seeds."

"Mi nombre es Miguel y tengo problemas con Seagram's Peach Tea Vodka." "

Mi nombre es Miguel y tengo problemas con snorting Well-butrin."

You get the point. Each night we'd do our best to try to make one another laugh as we drifted off to sleep. Then it just turned into crazy shit like, "Due to my sexual proclivities I am no longer allowed within 200 yards of a burn unit." The more nonsensical the better. Laughing that hard, to the point of my stomach aching, was something I hadn't experienced in ages. Not since before my addiction completely overtook my life had I laughed so hard. It gave me a glimmer of hope that perhaps it was possible to have fun sober. I just needed to, like Mike had described in group, surround myself with others as sick and twisted as me. It was the first step in experiencing the enjoyment that can be derived in recovery by simply connecting with another addict or alcoholic on a human level.

At the end of my 20+ days, my counselor, Adrienne, who rumor had it, used to be a probation officer, suggested that she thought I needed a "higher level of care." She thought I wasn't ready to be released back into the world. I was like WTF is a "higher level of treatment" than an inpatient, residential 28-day rehab? Now, to be fair, I did go out on pass one day the week prior for a doctor's appointment and told the group I had taken out money from the ATM to buy dope, but I didn't.

What actually happened was that on my way back from the doctor's appointment on the Pulaski blue line, I decided that if I was offered dope, I would grab a jab. I knew they would drop me (give me a drug test and/or breathalyzer) immediately after returning from a field trip, so I planned to put it up, wait until after I was tested, and then get busy. It didn't happen but it was clear that three weeks of treatment hadn't convinced me to refrain from using.

I think Adrienne didn't know what to do with me because I had nowhere to go when released. Generally, patients weren't discharged from rehab onto the streets. I would have to find a sober-living home or another program. Another option was a transitional program hosted on-site and down one floor. It was like an Intensive Outpatient Program (IOP) but you still lived within the confines of Gateway. You could work or go look for employment, but you had to attend group, return before 6:00 p.m. curfew, etc. I thought that would allow me to stack some paper up, have some accountability, and give me some time to figure out my longer-term plans. Without hesitation, she gave me a hard 'NO' on that idea. I was pissed. I had marinated the idea all weekend and thought she would be on board with it, but just like that, I was shut down.

Plenty of typical treatment-center antics went down during my stay, but the most interesting had to be on my second to last day. It was a Saturday, late morning. My three roommates and I found ourselves in our room just talking and bullshitting. After a few minutes, it became evident that each of us, all heroin addicts, still REALLY wanted to get high. The conversation quickly escalated from ideation to figuring out if there was some crazy way we could make this happen. One thing we had going for us was that one of our roommates had managed to sneak a cell phone into the facility during his admission process. In our eyes, the phone made it possible to come up with a plan, and we did.

The plan revolved around the Gateway smoke breaks that took place after group meetings and meals. Throughout the day, we got 12-15 trips outside near the back of the building, accompanied by a staff member, of course. But we still had to figure out how to make the logistics work, how to make an exchange with a supplier. The four of us peered out our window at the gazebo in back, trying to figure out if there was some way to pull this off.

First, we needed to find someone who could get some heroin and bring it to us. Our newest roommate mentioned that he had a buddy of his he could call and that he might be able to do it. We gave him a call and he said he was working most of the day but that he'd be off at 4:00 p.m.

Okay, cool. Now it was just a matter of figuring out how the handoff would work. The next few times we went out to smoke we surveyed the area for an option. Maybe the guy could put the dope on the wheel of a nearby car or in an empty chip bag and throw it in the garbage and we could retrieve it on the following smoke break. The main issue with this plan was the hour lag time between when he would leave it and our next smoke break. Plus, there were two other units at Gateway, and they were on a similar smoking schedule with breaks in the same area. What if one of them stumbled across our dope? What if they were outside on break when his friend arrived? We knew it was a long shot but the fact that his buddy was willing to do it gave us hope. I still had a couple hundred bucks on me from my field trip to the doctor's office, so money was not an issue. The issue was how to get it to him. One way or another we would figure it out.

Everyone had their idea and at one point it hit me. As we came in from the next smoke break, I checked the gas tank on one of the two conversion vans, aka "druggie buggies," parked just outside the back door. I thought if, and I mean if, we managed to convince the guy to help us out, I could leave money in the gas tank, and he could retrieve it and leave the dope behind. If I put out my cigarette before the others gathered to go back inside, I might have a moment to hide behind the van and pull it off. I thought it was pretty ingenious. When we got back inside, I described the plan to my roommates and of course, they were on board.

As 4:00 approached, we guarded the door so that our roommate could use the cell phone and coordinate the delivery. All the pieces were in place, but he didn't answer. Fuck. A text came in, "Still at work, off in an hour or so." Goddammit. Whatever. An hour went by, he texted that he didn't have a car and couldn't get a ride. What the fuck dude? Okay, we'll pay for an Uber. Long story short, he was full of excuses, and as hard as we tried to convince him, it wasn't gonna happen.

Epic deflate. The disappointment at that moment was palpable, I mean you could feel it. We were beyond frustrated. All day we had been basking in the thought of getting high and now that was shattered. Like all good junkies fiending for another one, we weren't going to accept our circumstances until we exhausted every single option.

There was a longshot option that I had been hesitant to offer up, but at this point, the gloom was so overwhelming that I was willing to give it a shot. I thought my guy Sam, who I'd been copping from for the last five years, might be able to help us out. Sam was cool, but aside from a few instances where I hopped in his car as he bent the corner while we transacted our business, the extent of our relationship consisted of car window-to-window handoffs. Asking him to smuggle heroin into a treatment center for us was beyond what even my closest junkie friends would be willing to do, even if they were dope sick and I offered to throw them a half jab. It was a pretty crazy ask, but the one glimmer of hope was that he lived no more than five minutes away.

Knowing he wouldn't pick up a call from an unknown number, I texted to tell him it was me calling on the phone and I asked if he was good (i.e., had dope). Within a couple of minutes he replied, so I gave him a call from the bathroom in our room while my room-mates stood guard near the door. Since I had been in the hospital and treatment for almost a month, it had been a while since I linked up with him. Rather than dick around, I just launched right into it. "Hey bro, you good?"

"Yeah man."

"Do you know where Gateway is at man, off of Taylor?"

"Yeah, you over near there?"
"Yeah, well, more specifically, I'm in Gateway bro. You think you could swing out this way and help me out?"

"You're in Gateway, oh shit, they let you use up in there?"
I chuckled, "Hell no man."
He laughed.

"We're fiending over here bro, is there any way that if I throw you a few extra bucks you could bring us a half jab?"
"How am I supposed to do that?"

"When you pull in, just drive to the back of the lot and turn right and there's a couple of vans parked there. I'll leave the money in the gas tank of the one on the left."
"Oh shit, they got cameras back there?"

They did, but I was not gonna tell him that. "Nah man."
"A'ight man."

Wait! Did he just say yes? Holy shit, I was fuckin' amped.

"When? Like now?"
"Come between 7:30 and 7:50 pm because we have a smoke break at 8:00 p.m. and that way I can grab it when I go out."
"A'ight cool man."

"Sweet, thank you bro, just text me once it's done."
"Cool." That was it and he hung up.

I exited the bathroom and had three sets of eyes fixated on me to hear the verdict. I said, "He's gonna do it."

There was brief elation and then we went right into planning mode, trying to figure out how we were gonna make this go seamlessly and get high come lights out.

It was just after 6:00 p.m. and our next smoke break would be around 7:00 p.m. I planned to wait for a moment when no one was watching and put the money in the gas tank, hoping nobody would be monitoring the cameras that were aimed directly at the area where the vans were parked. I figured that was the easy part. The first complication was hoping that Sam, running on typical slack-ass dope-man time, would show up during the designated time when none of the other units were outside. Second, how was I going to scoop the bags up from the tank during the smoke break while surrounded by a counselor and 20 other addicts?

There were so many things that could go wrong, but we were determined. We agreed that we'd wait until lights out to get high, so we wouldn't alert any of the other clients on the unit and wouldn't corrupt the folks who were invested in their recovery. We were to tell nobody else about the plan because if the staff caught wind of it, we'd probably be arrested, or at least kicked out. It was a risk we were all willing to take without hesitation.

Finally, it was time for our 7:00 p.m. smoke break. I finished my smoke early, popped the money in the gas tank and lined up by the door, no problem and we head back in.

"Did you do it?"

"Yeah, we're all set."

One of the other clients, Frankie, popped over to our room and asked my roommate if he could use his cell phone to call his girl. The roommate with the phone agreed. We looked at him like WTF? Why the fuck would you (1) be advertising to people that you had smuggled a phone in, (2) risk Frankie learning about our plan to carry off some crazy MacGyver type of shit, and (3) let Frankie tie up the phone when Sam might call or text us and we needed to have it available. We were floored that he could be so careless. Lucky for us, Frankie's girlfriend couldn't talk so he was off it relatively quickly, and we breathed a collective sigh of relief.

Random fact, three or four weeks later, I ran into Frankie at an NA meeting at Prince of Peace church in Addison. He asked me to piss in an empty water bottle for him as he was actively using, on probation, and trying to avoid violation. I was pissing clean at that point, and I reluctantly did it for him.

Anyway, as it approached 7:30 p.m. we were fixated on watching the parking lot through our bedroom window. The only area we couldn't see was around the corner where the vans were parked. We were all thinking about how this could go wrong. What if they had to pick up a new client and they took the van? What if someone noticed the car driving up? Except for someone leaving at the end of their shift, there wasn't a good reason for a car to drive up to Gateway at that hour on Saturday night. What if the adult female unit or the Partial Hospitalization Program (PHP) groups happened to be out for a smoke when he came in? Our entire plan would be foiled as he'd find twenty people back there smoking.

One roommate, Jason, was so overcome by anxiety that he perched on the windowsill staring outside and watching for headlights and Sam's car. We begged him to relax and play it cool; we thought he might blow our cover.

At one point, another client did say, "Bro, why's he plastered up there staring outside?"

I said the only thing that came to mind, "Dude, he just got out of jail and he's all obsessed with nature and shit and can't get enough of it." Pretty lame, but it got rid of the guy.

When it was almost 7:45 p.m. we knew our window of opportunity was closing. I called Sam. Straight to voicemail. Fuck. I tried two more times, the same thing. Shit. WTF? I come out of the bathroom for a moment. Someone noticed a car pulling into the lot.

"Hey, hey, what kind of car does he drive?"
"A black Jeep Cherokee. Why, do you see him?"
"Nah man. It's not a Jeep."

The car parked and left its lights on. One of the counselors from our unit walked out to the car, got in and they just sat there. A couple of minutes go by. Fuck, what's going on? If Sam shows up now and this guy sees a car pull around to the back of the building, it's going to raise all kinds of suspicions.

Back to the bathroom and I call again. It rang a couple of times, but no answer.

"Another car's coming."

"Is it a jeep?"

"Might be. Wait yeah, I think it is, it is man."

The car pulled six or seven spaces past the other car and parked next to one of the white vans. The wrong white van. It was Sam. What the fuck was he doing. I was very specific that it's around the back of the building. The phone vibrated, it's him. "I'm here bro."

"Yeah, I can see you man, but the van is in the back. You need to go down another 50 yards and bend the corner."

"Oh okay, I got you."

He disappeared beyond our sightline and no more than 30 seconds later he pulled away.

"Did he do it?"

"I assume so."

I had asked him to text us "done" to confirm it was done. A few minutes later it came. One word. One syllable and I was ecstatic. One of the guys said, "I bet he stole your money." The thought had never crossed my mind. Maybe the dudes this guy dealt with were scandalous drug dealers, but I trusted Sam and had been going to him for years. If he went through all this trouble to make it happen, it wasn't just so he could get over on me for $60 bucks.

Our plan was pretty simple. My roommate would aim to be first in line for smoke break and hustle out the doors five to six steps ahead of everyone, quickly retrieve the heroin, and that was that. It all went as planned and he was the first one out, with everyone else trailing him. Once everyone was outside, he gave us a nod of acknowledgment to let us know it was good.

He came over and told me, "Dude, there were only four in there."
"Are you sure?"

He's felt around in his pocket. "There's only four."
"Then you missed two man, you gotta get 'em."

He used the same method I used to deposit the funds. Extinguished his smoke early and checked the tank. Sure enough, he missed two the first time.

"All good?"
"Yep, we're good," and we headed back up.

The waiting was the hardest part and we had almost two hours until lights out. After the emotional rollercoaster of the day, just knowing we would get blasted soon felt unbelievable.

After having been clean for almost a month, that shit kicked our ass. We were all sorts of fucked up. It was a legit party in room #306 for a couple of hours past lights out. We had two-man teams taking turns snorting dope in the bathroom while the others kept an eye out for staff. Seeing as I orchestrated this whole plan and funded this nonsense, I felt entitled to a bit more than everyone else. Apparently, I did like three times more than everyone else and the next morning I was a hot mess.

They physically couldn't get me out of bed for group and the last thing any of us wanted was to draw suspicion from staff. I was

ROBERT J. KUBIAK JR.

normally up at the butt crack of dawn. By 6:00 a.m. I would be showered and drinking coffee in the dayroom, waiting for the first smoke break of the day. But not today. They brought me a cup of coffee to try to help wake me up, but I was in full-on dope fiend, nod-mode and I spilled it all over myself. They tried again, but it just wasn't happening.

Breakfast was optional at Gateway, so they left me to sleep. I also missed the check-in group that morning. With over 25 clients on the unit, it might go unnoticed. No harm, no foul.

As time for the first group approached, they got worried. "You can't miss group man, or they'll know something's up."

They urged me to appear attentive and awake. I remember being so goddamn high and uncomfortable trying not to appear fucked up, but the specifics of how that played out escape me now. Then, in the middle of group, Adrienne called me out to meet with her in her office. She gave me the specifics on where I'd be going once I was discharged, when I was going to be picked up, and all that jazz. I remember struggling to stay awake and appear okay.

Then she said in her stern voice, "Robert, (she called me Robert), Robert, are you high? Are you high right now?"

"No, what are you talking about?"
"You look high."

Of course, I denied, denied, denied. I think at that point she knew, but with only a few hours until discharge, she just wanted to get me off Gateway's hands. She left it alone. I remember asking if

I'd be getting a certificate of completion and some Gateway swag. Not sure why that was of concern to me at that very moment, but apparently the tote bag, t-shirt, and certificate were important to my heroin-faded ass.

The next thing I remember is being told that my ride was here. I dapped up with several of the clients, grabbed my tote bag and the garbage bag that held the few articles of clothes I had with me, and walked out the front doors greeted by yet another white van.

"Rob?"
"Yep."

"I'm Cornell. Hi, how are you doing?" And with that, we were off.

I could have left Gateway for Footprints to Recovery with 24 days of clean time, but instead, I had less than 24 hours. When I arrived at intake the staff was shocked to learn that I was testing positive for opiates. "How do you come directly from a treatment center and test positive?"

Without even thinking of the potential consequences or that they may not accept me if I were still under the influence. I said, "Lemme tell ya a little story."

-

8

# Mayweather vs McGregor
# (Fight Night)

*Listening to the subdued tones of confined jazz*
*Forever imprisoned by both form and parameter*
*Sweating on a tattered rug in a fit of anxiety*
*Taking a slow dive into a fictitious dimension momentarily*
*And throwing it all away recklessly*

In August of 2017 there was a fair amount of hype surrounding the "Money Fight" also known as the "Biggest Fight in Combat Sports History." It was a professional boxing match between undefeated 11-time, five-division boxing world champion Floyd Mayweather Jr. and two-division Mixed Martial Arts (MMA) world champion and Ultimate Fighting Championship (UFC) Lightweight Champion, Conor McGregor. The fight was scheduled at T-Mobile Arena in Paradise, Nevada, on August 26. It would be 12 rounds and the second-highest pay-per-view buy rate in history. I don't give a shit about boxing or MMA, but I was in rehab at the

8

time and there was a lot of chatter amongst my fellow patients about who was going to win.

That week I surpassed 50 consecutive days clean for the first time in more than two years, but I was still plagued by an intense desire to get high. I was living at a halfway house called Normandy House in Des Plaines, Illinois, and attending an IOP at Footprints to Recovery. I had been at Normandy for a couple of weeks, kind of against my will. My insurance benefits had run out and would no longer cover the housing costs for me to stay at the residential portion of Footprints in the Townplace Suites by Marriott. I had written a heartfelt letter to corporate pleading with them to allow me to stay in housing and asked if there was anything they could do, a scholarship perhaps, to allow my stay to be extended. I did not feel ready to be out on my own and had serious concerns about relapsing. I received no response. I had to find somewhere else to live and to Footprint's credit, they went way beyond the extra mile to help facilitate my recovery.

Knowing I had no car or transportation, they would send a van to pick me up each morning from Normandy House. They'd bring me to the hotel and transport me around with the rest of the clients to clinical for groups during the morning and afternoon and then to an AA or NA meeting each night. At the end of the day, they would drop me off back in Des Plaines. I felt so grateful that they were willing to do that for me; it was a testament to the lengths they were willing to go to help me stay clean.

On Friday, August 25th, I was smoking a Newport on the patio outside of the Marriott shortly before we would be leaving for an AA meeting. Out of nowhere, I had an unbelievably strong desire to overdose and end things. It was intense. Part of the reason for that feeling was that I was uncomfortable having been uprooted from my fellow patients at housing, several of whom I had become very close with. I was still acclimating to the new community at Normandy House. I hated being dropped back off each evening and returning to the still unfamiliar surroundings.

The camaraderie at the halfway house was nowhere close to what I had in residential housing. Everybody seemed to be doing their own thing and they would leave for work during the day. I saw people congregating in the evening in the driveway, hanging out and smoking and catching up, but I felt disconnected; like an outsider with a dirty little secret that I still REALLY wanted to use.

I don't remember much about the meeting that night, but on the van ride home I started talking about how I seriously felt like I was on the verge of a relapse. A few of the other clients asked if I had called my sponsor, which, of course, I hadn't. I still hadn't even chosen between AA or NA. I had been loitering around the edge of both groups, reviewing the literature, etc. I had full-blown paralysis of analysis and a lack of willingness to commit to doing the work to recover. I hadn't been willing to lean into the discomfort and get a sponsor and be held accountable for my own recovery.

About five years prior at the Harvey 100 Club, I had gone through the same charade and described it to a guy named Wade, who was a mentor of sorts for me at the time. He'd been listening to me drone on for weeks about how I was unable to make up my mind about which program to work, which job to take, where to live, and a host of other things. I'd rather spend time marinating the pros and cons of every single possible option and outcome. One day he abruptly interrupted. He said, "Rob, indecision IS a decision. Just DO something." Damn. That hit me hard and blew my wig back. I was like, fuck man, he's right. Spot-on. That night as I rode the van back complaining about how I felt like I'm gonna relapse, I clearly remembered that conversation with Wade. Unfortunately, it didn't change the path I was on.

Since moving to Normandy House, I had a routine for Saturday morning— I would catch the first bus from downtown Des Plaines over to Woodfield Mall. I'd hop off and walk over to the Townplace Suites, which was just a 15-minute walk. For the past couple of months, they had been taking any clients that wanted to attend to an 8:30 am morning meeting at the West Suburban Alano Club (WSAC) in Westmont, and for the past couple of weeks, they had been more than happy to allow me to tag along. For whatever reason, that morning, nobody had decided to get up early to voluntarily make it to the van for the 7:30 am departure time, so there was no meeting that morning.

It was a nice, sunny morning, so I headed to the back patio with my journal. After an hour or so of journaling, I threw on my headphones, took off my hoodie, and lay down on the couch to get some sun. I may have nodded off and was startled when my phone vibrated. It was Megan, a fellow client, who had a relapse or "slip," a couple of days prior. It was just a one-time, one-day thing, but they removed her from housing. She was back home staying with her parents and commuting to clinical for group on weekdays.

I met Megan at Footprints where she arrived a week or so after I did. She was a 21-year-old recovering heroin addict who was in her final year of undergraduate at Loyola University. Megan, me, and

Dustin, who had recently been discharged, were close friends during our stay there. I'm also relatively certain the two of them were hooking up on the low. Megan was like a surrogate younger sister, and I would periodically, and not so subtly, remind her how important it was to just get through her last year of school and stay clean. I told her that after that if she wanted to indulge, then go ahead because I know how difficult it is for a 21-year-old to fathom staying clean for the rest of their life. But I also know how difficult it is to return to school after taking a year off for rehab. I didn't want her to fall into that trap. I hadn't seen her since her relapse, other than for a brief moment smoking a cigarette the day before at clinical. She was shaken up about the discharge and cagy about the details, so I was eager to chat and hear how she was doing.

After exchanging pleasantries, Megan told me that a mutual friend of ours, Liz, also recently discharged from Footprints to Recovery, called her all fucked up and had been up all-night drinking and doing coke. Liz was by herself at some random bar out in Hillside. She had asked Megan for my dope dealer's number and claimed she wanted to do some heroin. We knew she hadn't tried heroin before. Megan didn't know what to do. Fuck man, it was my first couple weeks out of housing, I was on the brink of relapsing, and now I was in the middle of this crazy predicament. I lit up a Newport 'cuz this was something I needed to smoke about.

Megan and I talked and concluded that she was stranded and lonely, and just wanted someone to scoop her up and keep the party going. I decided to give Liz a call and try to talk her off the ledge. Within a minute or two she confirmed our suspicions and it was clear she was looking for someone, anyone, to help her continue to escape from herself. I know that feeling all too well. Rather than offer her an answer, I told her I'd give my guy a call and get back to her. This bought some time for me to get back with Megan and figure out what to do. I suggested we simply tell her that he wasn't picking up and that we'd keep trying him until we got through. Sounded like a legit plan. Megan called her back to let her know.

The problem was that upon hearing the news, Liz was like, fuck it, and she was going to just take an Uber to the West Side. The West Side of Chicago is not a good place for a young fucked-up woman to be by herself. Eventually, Megan agreed to pick her up to prevent her from getting herself in trouble. I was thinking to myself, would Liz really have taken an Uber to the West Side to try to go cop dope? Shit, she probably didn't even know where the West Side was. Megan asked me if I wanted to come with. We didn't say it, but we each sensed that the other wanted to get high, even though I was closing in on 60 days clean. After a bit of back and forth, I said that if she was going to go get Liz that she better come pick me up.

I sat there waiting for Megan, my mind racing, and my heart fluttering. I was conflicted about what to do. It's at this point that an addict should pick up their phone and call their sponsor or some-one in the program. You tell on yourself. But for me, once I got that urge, the entire program, a sponsor, coping skills, and everything I've learned over the years went right out the fucking window. The "switch" hadn't been fully flipped but while I was chain-smoking on the back patio waiting for Megan, I was thinking about how nice a couple of blows (snorting heroin) would be.

I got in the car with Megan and we both knew that we were going to get high. Even if we talked Liz out of it, and convinced her not to do dope, we both fully intended to use ourselves. We pulled up to this seedy, roadhouse-looking bar and Liz scrambled out and hopped in the backseat. She was in the outfit she had worn the night before and her makeup was smudged just enough to show that she hadn't slept. She was talking a million miles a minute, trying to catch us up on 48 hours' worth of information in three minutes. We were trying to process all of this while subtly glancing at one another, smirking about the absurdity of her story. She concluded by saying that before we did anything we gotta go to McDonald's. Sounds good, we'll get some food in her, maybe she'll just pass out, and we can just drop her off at home so she can get some much-needed rest.

Never in my life had I seen a 105-pound human being inhale $14.76 worth of McDonald's in approximately eight minutes, but I guess there's a first time for everything. The food seemed to re-energize her and fueled her demand to get some dope. Now, I don't know if you've ever tried to talk a drunk 21-year-old female out of doing something, but it's safe to say that nobody's been successfully able to do such a thing since like 1867 A.D. Neither Megan nor I were putting up much of a fight to curb her craving. The switch had been flipped for ol' Roberto and within minutes I was on the phone with my guy Sam.

He said he would meet us just off Ogden and Randolph by the McDonalds. I felt a brief twinge of guilt about turning someone onto dope, but over the years I've turned countless others onto weed, pills, ecstasy, cocaine – you name it. One of them, Hans, was one of my roommates sophomore year. Years later he murdered a doctor in the Gold Coast who had prescribed Accutane for him, and he became convinced it made him impotent. After a crazy manhunt that was all over the news, he was caught, and last I heard, he is serving life in prison. I figured a little toot of heroin for Liz probably wasn't the worst thing I had ever done, and given her current state, she'd probably just fall asleep.

We got there before Sam, who was running on dope dealer time today even though he was usually relatively prompt. I saw his black Jeep Cherokee and we followed it half a block and into an alley. We pulled alongside for the hand-off, rolled down the window, and realized we had followed the wrong car. It was some poor woman who was probably wondering what the hell we wanted. For lack of a better response, I said, "Hi there," Megan threw it in reverse, and we headed back to the lot across from McDonald's. Damn, talk about your all-time backfires. I felt like an idiot and tried to explain to them that he has the exact same car and that busting down a nearby alley was generally how we'd do it. Shit.

A few minutes later, Sam called and said he was just across the street. This time Megan followed the correct car down the same alley, and we transacted our business. We pulled away with a jab (12 bags of heroin, $100) inside of 30 seconds. Always nice and smooth with Sam. We rolled out, found a non-descript parking spot a few blocks away and got down to business. Megan chopped up lines for us, ensuring that Liz didn't get too much. The past five months' worth of treatment vernacular started circulating in my head. I started feeling guilty again. Fucking-A man! I know I knew better, but fuck. I didn't know what to do. Megan handed me the straw and I briefly contemplated the plethora of repercussions I would have to endure, but fuck it, I took care of business. Ahh. Wow. This feeling is why I LOVE dope. Why I always come back to it.

Now that we've all gotten right, what should we do? I figured at some point we had got to get Liz back home to Naperville. Aside from that, I was content doing whatever, just as long as it involved a few more blows. Megan was on the same page and hopped back on I-290 West toward the suburbs so we could dump Liz off. I was justifying this as a "sobriety vacation," and since I had started, I figured go big or go home. Perhaps we could make this a monthly or bi-monthly thing. We could take a day or two off from being clean and get our sick off. I shared the idea with Megan and Liz, it sounded like a splendid plan to all three of our doped-up asses. That called for another bag apiece, so we got down again.

As I held the wheel for Megan to do hers, she started tripping out. It just occurred to her that when she got back home, her mom was 100% going to drop (drug-test) her. Jesus fuck! This would have been good to know two hours before when I was balls deep in fifty-one days' worth of crystal clean urine. I easily could have bottled some piss up for her forgetful ass before we started snorting heroin. Motherfucker. Called for another blow to figure something out.

Shit, all three of us knew like 40 people with clean urine still in treatment at Footprints over at the Townplace Suites back in Schaumburg. Okay, cool. We could find someone there to piss in a bottle for her on the way back. Easier said than done. Apparently, those former junkies, drunks, and pill poppers were taking this "working an honest program" bullshit a little too literally. We called or texted 10 or 12 people, who all respectfully declined. That included Liz's current "boyfriend" and that really set her off. Eventually, after a little begging and pleading, we found a kind soul, Tim, whose own recovery was questionable at best, who was willing to help a girl out.

After another nasal blast to reward ourselves for sorting that out, we made our way to the Townplace Suites. By now, I was thoroughly high but didn't want to advertise this to the people who were still in treatment. When we got near the hotel, I told Megan to drop Liz and me off across the street at the Homewood Suites while she crossed the street to cop that piss from Tim. We post-up outside and light up a square. Ahh, yes. My god. A Newport after I toot or shoot some dope might be one of my favorite things on this planet.

Liz sat on the curb and decided it was time to call her rehab boy-friend, and my former roommate, Nevan. She decided this was the perfect time to get into a petty fight over some nonsense and within minutes the water works started. Okay wonderful, just what I signed up for. Shit. At this point I noticed a guy near us standing beside his red pickup truck with what I assumed was his girlfriend, clearly eavesdropping on us. They started wandering in our direction and I noticed he was drinking. He asked us if we want a beer. I'm not a big drinker, so I said, "No thanks," but Liz gladly accepted one. She was drinking between talking on the phone and wiping tears away.

He introduced himself as Malo and told me the girl's name, but it escapes me now. I said, "Malo? Like 'bad' in Spanish?" He nodded and I introduced myself and Liz and we got to chatting and bullshitting. I swear, inside of two minutes, in not so many words, he asked me if we want to have a foursome. I was like, what the fuck? I couldn't help but chuckle, thinking if he only knew our circumstances and exactly what we were doing there. Because I was high as fuck, I decided to enlighten him, and surprisingly, he wasn't remotely phased by its absurdity. He said that they were all coked up, out of their minds and asked again if Liz might want to hook up with his girlfriend. I didn't know, maybe she did. She used to strip

ROBERT J. KUBIAK JR.

and was a go-go dancer, but I didn't know if she was bi? So, I said, "Ask her, maybe she's game."

At this point, I was wondering if everything went smoothly for Megan, so I gave her a shout. No answer. Shot her a quick text. Nothing. What the fuck? I hope some shit didn't backfire and Tim got caught trying to bring his own urine out to Megan. Then I hear Malo mention that he just picked up a bunch of raw heroin and if we knew anyone that might be interested in some dope? Holy shit! If only this motherfucker knew there were 45 or so people across the street that were all ripe for relapse. For once, I used my better judgment and refrained from disclosing this information. However, I was fucking game to try some of this aforementioned uncut raw. I tried Megan again and still no answer. My phone was about to die, and Malo said he had an Android charger in their room and invited us back with them. I was a bit anxious as I had known these two for all of eight minutes. But I went along and plugged my phone in. Liz looked perfectly content, guzzling a Modelo and chatting with the girl. Malo said again that he was trying to unload a bunch of raw dope and I couldn't charge my phone fast enough. How was this happening?

I kept trying Megan and, finally, after 30-45 minutes, it became clear that she wasn't coming back. Straight fucking ditched us, knowing Liz needed to get to Naperville and that I needed to make my way back to the recovery home before curfew. I decided to head to the bus depot a mile or so up the road and get back to Des Plaines. I asked Liz what she wanted to do. Evidently, Liz and Malo's girlfriend had hit it off. Without hesitation, Liz said, "I'm gonna stay here."

| 90 |

"You sure?"

"Yep, I'm good."

"Well okay, cool, I'm gonna get going."

Malo offered me a ride up to the bus station. I was still apprehensive about him. Obviously, this dude wasn't exactly a fine upstanding citizen, but neither was I. But could I trust him? Was he going to take me to the bus station, or would he take a detour and I would find myself in a seedy motel bathtub full of ice with my spleen removed and a ransom note or some crazy shit? That was just my addict mind running on overdrive, and he simply dropped me off at the station. We exchanged numbers before we parted ways. I got back to Normandy House around 10:00 p.m. or so, still high as fuck. I snuck in quietly and since most of the other guys were cheering and watching the pay-per-view fight in the large meeting room upstairs, I made it in completely unscathed. Nobody knew. It was an incredible relief to have gotten away with getting high, sliding back home and into bed and nobody was the wiser. It was great.

I woke up, or came to, the next morning around 10:45 a.m., grabbed my cell phone off the charger and texted Megan to find out what the hell happened to her. She called me quickly and was uber-apologetic about ditching us in Schaumburg. She said she had to get right back home to avoid suspicion from her parents and couldn't take the time to drop both of us off at our respective homes. If she had been late or if she dropped dirty, she would have been kicked out, so I understood why she did what she did. After I told her what I was able to remember about our little adventure, she felt less guilty about bailing on us.

She asked what had happened with Liz and I said she seemed perfectly happy to stay. I hadn't called or texted her yet and I nervously shot her a quick text asking her if she was okay while I was chatting with Megan. I immediately got back a "great time" followed by four smiley face emojis. Okay then, no harm, no foul. At least all my peeps were accounted for, and things seemed to work out okay for everyone. Solid. I thought again about how this could be a monthly thing for us, and I drifted back to sleep for another hour or two.

I don't know what you were doing the night of the "Money Fight" or if you happened to catch it and see Mayweather beat McGregor with a technical knock-out (TKO) in the 10th round, but that's what I was up to. I felt like we got away with it and came out completely intact despite a crazy series of events, but I was way wrong. Within 10 days, my entire world would be turned upside down. By September 7th, our escapade was discovered by the staff at Footprints, and I found out that the girl with Malo that night had hung herself and committed suicide. I was kicked out of treatment, again, and overdosed in the middle of the student union at Loyola University. I found myself charging my phone in the outdoor outlet on the side of a McDonald's in Des Plaines. It was directly across from the first-ever Mcdonald's, which has since been torn down. I stood there, juicing my phone up just enough to make a call.

"Hello, Banyan Treatment Center? Yeah, so I just overdosed, got kicked out of my recovery home, and I need help."

# 9

# South Bender

*Feeling obtuse enlightenment amongst the mentally ill*
*This trip will take us to an entirely new realm*
*Some of us won't be adept at adapting to the new surroundings*
*A small star in the solar system emanates gloriously bright hope*
*Sometimes these things go unnoticed – and continued patterns are*
*maintained*
*Metaphysical nothingness traps the emotionally distraught*
*Forever restricted to defined parameters inflicted upon oneself*
*Dormant obsessions never to be reawakened flounder to some non-*
*existent plane*
*Burying your experience in graveyards of lost thought*
*Surrendering to the upheaval because of pure ambivalence*
*The submission is subtle, but its effect is most profound*
*Surreptitious lies hover amidst the puddles of murky opportunities*
*Terrified of reconstructions of reality and the unknown fasci-*
*nations within*
*Trapped in a state of static existence for undetermined durations*
*The frustration alone is enough to entirely overcome a man*
*Fleeting hope prances by, but is unnoticed by most*

*As they're buried amongst broken dreams and false promises*
*Imprisoned by time and archaic fallacies contribute to the wisdom*
*gained*
*Echoes of yesterday emanate today and have a repetitive vibe*
*Tragic young men and women are losing conscious contact with*
*reality*
*Hiding amidst the medicated confines of safety and inactivity*
*You develop a new, institutionalized sanity that's difficult to*
*describe*
*Or even to ascertain – but it's there.*

Before Banyan Treatment Center in Naperville would accept me, I had to spend a week in detox at a less than stellar facility called Choices on the outskirts of South Bend, Indiana. I met a bearded fellow there, Jon, who was from Villa Park. We had both been given the same description of Choices by an admissions operator over the phone. She made it seem like it was a paradise and something like a *Passages of Malibu*. We were told they had their own private chef and nutritionist, a hot tub, on-site masseuse, gardens, and their own private health club. Okay, let me break this down for ya. The detox unit was kept at what felt like 57 degrees Fahrenheit and I was constantly freezing. The bed frame and box spring jacked up my back terribly. The "private chef" was a group of former clients, hired for $10/hour to cook in a kitchen that no health department in the history of health departments would deem fit for food preparation. The hot tub was a cheap, outdoor tub filled with their hose and fenced-in. It hadn't been working in months. The "gardens" were a client-created hodge-podge of baby tomatoes and random flowers and plants. It wasn't what one would describe as "well-kept." The health club was a rubber-floored area with miscellaneous exercise machines, free weights, and a ping pong table. It was probably the nicest portion of the facility, the rest of which resembled an old pre-school or kindergarten.

The best part of the entire experience was the massage therapist even though he was not an actual masseuse. Instead, he was a Native American fellow who gave what they so eloquently referred to as "assists," which resembled something between a shoulder rub and inappropriate touching. At times, he would be walking by and give you an impromptu "assist" that certainly caught you off guard.

To top things off, the small kitchen area in the detox unit was littered with fruit flies. I mean, you'd literally open a cabinet and flies would fly out. It was anything but what it was built up to be, but the dismal conditions provided us with something to chit-chat about while we were between groups or out having a smoke or a vape in Jon's case. Nothing brings people together like a common enemy.

When we were ready to be transferred to Banyan in Naperville, I could tell Jon had a lot of anxiety, this being his first time in treatment. I tried to assure him that Banyan would be drastically different from our brief South Bender, despite not knowing for sure what to expect myself. During the transfer, we met another fellow named Jon, in a miscellaneous McDonald's parking lot near Merrillville, IN, halfway between Chicago and South Bend. I quickly chiefed a Newport. The last Newport I had, and we were off.

All I knew of Banyan was from comments I overheard during my stint at Footprints to Recovery. I've learned that you can generally trust other addicts' descriptions of treatment facilities and their conditions. However, that's about all you can trust from them.

About an hour and a half later we arrived in a parking garage some-where in downtown Naperville and hopped out of the van with our belongings. We walked up a back stairwell to the second floor of a non-descript building referred to as the Main Street Promenade. The intake process was standard. The usual drug history, family relations, brief psychological review to ensure you're not going to harm yourself or anyone else, understanding of the program, and explanation of fees. No sweat. I assumed the office we were in was where groups were held, more commonly referred to as "clinical." The housing component was off-site and having just been to a treatment center at a Marriott hotel, I anticipated a severe down-grade in both amenities and accommodations. Turned out, they owned a couple of apartment buildings a few miles from downtown 'NaperThrill'. Pretty standard two-bedroom, fully furnished, rela-tively large, and two per room. They asked us what we wanted from Subway and a skinny, older black gentleman (Billy) returned shortly thereafter with our grub. Jon flipped on the television and so began our Banyan adventure.

When we arrived, the rest of the residents were out at a meeting, and Jon and I were the only two in our apartment. I knew at some point they would be calling me down for evening meds, at which point I would have my first opportunity to see what kind of card I'd been dealt on the fellow client front. I've been in and out of treatment so many times, that it wouldn't surprise me if I ran into someone I knew from a previous stint in rehab.

Later that evening, I was sitting in the dayroom with a handful of clients. It was the living room of a one-bedroom apartment that had been converted into a med-line waiting room. I was scanning the room to see if I recognized anyone; I didn't. We started doing the awkward intro thing and it turned out that one of these characters grew up in Lake Zurich, which is the town next to where I grew up in Barrington. He was a year older than me, and we started playing the "do you know so-and-so" game. Within minutes, we were swapping stories about a mutual friend, Holden, who he hadn't seen since high school and whom I didn't meet until several years after that. I filled him in on what Holden had been up to. I'll spare you the details about Holden for now, because he truly deserves his own novel with all the crazy shit that dude managed to get himself into in his time on this planet. Anyway, after that brief exchange, I was finally able to exhale a bit, feel at home again, and began settling into my new surroundings.

Arriving at treatment on the weekend has both its positives and its negatives, depending on what sort of condition you arrive in. Having been in uninterrupted treatment for the last 100 days or so, I was anxious to get rolling and get a feel for what the clinical situation would be like.

I wanted to meet my counselor and start emotionally manipulating them so that I could be earmarked for an expedited advancement to an IOP. I had a job (barely), but that was it. I was desperately clinging to that because it was the only thing keeping me from killing myself.

I also wanted to start group meetings so I could get all the details on my fellow clients and see where they were coming from. At this point in my life, I was completely comfortable sharing and telling complete strangers any and everything about myself. I would divulge shit you generally wouldn't tell your closest friends. Crazy because

ROBERT J. KUBIAK JR.

outside of treatment, you'd be hard-pressed to get me to even call and order a pizza because I would have to interact with a stranger.

It's funny how the scariest thing in the world for an addict is to try to go through normal life—to do all the mundane shit that every other human being does on a daily basis. It's terrifying.

Early on at Banyan, I was all ears, listening and jumping to conclusions about every single person. There was always an acclimation period when I arrived at a facility when I could casually eavesdrop on conversations and get a sense of the environment. As much as I didn't want to admit it, I would make assumptions as I took inventory of the clients. For example, I looked for the non-smokers. People who don't smoke at rehab trip me out and I would look for an explanation. I learned that, typically, they are the nicest and most soft-spoken individuals at treatment.

I analyzed people before they even opened their mouth based on their outfits, mannerisms, haircut, disposition, energy level, attentiveness, number of visible tattoos and piercings. As an aside, I can tell you that addicts have a proliferation of ink. Seems like every addict has tattoos, and in that regard, I was in the minority being both ink and piercing-free. I could also tell that my cohort Jon was very uncomfortable in this environment, and I don't blame him. I'm sure it was as foreign to him as my first rehab rodeo back in 1999 was to me.

We went around the room and there was a diverse group of individuals with a fair share of junkies, so I felt right at home. I could immediately identify the seasoned treatment veterans. I could sense who was there for legal issues, who was there because of their folks or their spouse or their children. Who was there for depression, anxiety, or simply because they had nowhere else to go. I guess the latter was my predicament, although I was sort of masquerading and pretending that I wanted help with my addiction. Truth was, I was all out of options. I was teetering on the brink of whether or not to kill myself or buy into the program, fall into line, and see what happened.

I positioned myself as a treatment veteran, having been doing it for years and I was quite comfortable amidst all the chaos, vulnerability, and uncertainty. I had spent 100 days in treatment and found myself here because of a little hiccup with heroin. Hopefully, they would allow me to resume the work arrangement I had during my stay at Footprints.

Time was of the essence because I was skating on thin ice on the employment front. I had been since I was out of my mind doped up and giving a speech at our company party back in December 2014. The last four years had been a pattern of rehab, using again, relapse, repeat, with the consequences getting progressively more severe. I was preoccupied with keeping my job, everything else was white noise. I was just going through the motions, playing the part of the well-adjusted client.

The next day, I met my counselor, Vanessa. She was NOT on the same page regarding my proposed treatment plan. It infuriated me but I tried not to show it. I made a plan to emotionally manipulate her so she would change her mind, or at least, open up to bargaining. Despite my pleas and empty threats, it became clear that she wasn't going to budge. I tried to determine who the fuck oversaw this place so I could go over her head. Surely, they would understand my situation and overrule this bitch and give me what I wanted. Not so much. Game, set, match – Banyan.

I was looking at a minimum of 45 days in PHP, and that was that. If I didn't want to comply, I could leave. With $34 and three packs of Newports, I wasn't going to get very far. So, I did what any addict would do and bitched about it incessantly to anyone who would listen. I isolated myself and exhausted all my mental equity pining about it until I drifted off into a restless sleep. I hoped for the best but expected the worst.

I asked my counselor to contact my boss and let him know of my current predicament. She agreed, provided we did it together over a conference call. I got the "just concerned about you" spiel from him. He was glad I was okay but wanted to know when I would be able to start working again. That was a TBD by Vanessa, but she said it wouldn't be for at least a month. I could hear the disappointment on the other end of the phone, but it was what it was.

With no work, I focused on what was going on around me. My frustration had been clouding my reality so intensely that, at 10 days in, I was still trying to acclimate. I still wasn't sharing much during group and had mostly buried my head in my journal. I started getting comfortable during a goodbye ceremony one day. They have a jarring routine at discharge and, I mean literally, they give you a jar filled with several items and a note, explaining the purpose of the items in the jar.

It includes:

Candle to light your way when things get dark

Band-aid to heal your wounds
Paperclip to help you keep things together
Pen & paper to share your thoughts
Star to remind you to keep shining
Eraser to fix the little mistakes
Penny so you always know you have worth
Rubber band to help you stretch beyond your limits
Heart to remind you to remain lovable
Key chain so you can keep the serenity prayer with you
Our phone number so you know help is only a call away

At about this time, while shaving one morning, I decided to consider taking booty juice (Vivitrol). It's a monthly shot that blocks your opiate receptors and prevents you from being able to get high. It was also supposed to help with cravings. I had always balked at the idea because I knew I would want to use again, and I wouldn't want to wait 3-4 weeks for it to wear off. But now I looked at it as an insurance policy for early recovery.

The next day, a couple of guys came to housing and did an in-house AA meeting called a "bridge group." I asked one of the guys to be my sponsor. This was totally out of character for me; I had never had a legit sponsor before. I had a suspicion that this recovery might be different and the start of something special. I even jotted it down in my journal. But exactly one week later, on September 27th, my world was upended.

My counselor told me that she had spoken to my boss, and I had been fired. It shouldn't have come as any surprise, but that was the only thing, the last thing, that I was hanging onto. I had nothing else, and it crushed me. It destroyed my spirit and all I could think about was putting a shotgun in my mouth and ending what I had started 18 years earlier when I took a knife to my wrist back in college. Since then, I had fleeting periods of okay-ed-ness, followed by longer periods of sinking into the abyss of hell and circling the drain with whatever substance I was abusing at the time. I was tired of the eloquent bullshit existence I was stumbling through. When I was younger, I could do it, but I didn't have the give-a-shit-ed-ness to make another go of treatment and sobriety and all that goes with it. I was miserable and just buying time until I ended my life. It would be my grand finale, well, actually, it would be more of a murmur. I didn't feel involved in my treatment plan. I became completely disengaged and made no effort to disguise my contempt for my current circumstances.

A few days earlier during group they had handed out the only real piece of homework in rehab – writing your life story/autobiography. Most people write a couple of pages or make an outline with some bullet points on a sheet of paper. In a couple of weeks, we would present it to the group. I love to write, so this was right up my alley.

I remember toying with the idea of writing it as an obituary instead of an autobiography, but after discussing my idea with a few other patients, the consensus was that it might lead me to a different kind of treatment facility. Fuck that. I threw myself into the assignment and it gave me something resembling a sense of purpose. It kept me occupied so I didn't fall off the deep end. I spent damn near every minute of free time I had scribbling vigorously in the spiralbound notebook they had provided. When all was said and done, I ended up with 23 pages. It was like an abridged "rob 37 heroin" starting from childhood, straight up until the present. It didn't change my current predicament, but it was a welcome distraction. I read the entire thing, verbatim, to the group. It took over an hour and one of the counselors whom I admired and respected, asked if he could photocopy it. That shit carried me for days man. It was one of the greatest unspoken compliments I've ever received.

I don't know if it was the acceptance of my story by my fellow rehabbers, the cravings being curbed by the Vivitrol, working the 12 steps with a sponsor, or what, but I started to snap out of the funk that had been my status quo since finding out I lost my job. It was at that point that I started connecting with the great group of guys and gals that were there at the time. Those treatment moments and the multitude of ways and levels you connect with people is something I can only equate to being a freshman in a college dorm. It's fun and exciting and you're away from your family and friends. In rehab, you're together 24 hours a day for 30-60 days and you get to know one another intimately.

They say the opposite of addiction is connection and I started seeing noticeable changes once I started letting people in. Those shared experiences were powerful, and I made some incredible friends on my journey—six or seven of whom are still sober more than four years later. That is an unheard-of type of success.

It was around this time that I was wrapping up PHP and would be moving over to IOP, which meant I'd have my days free and only needed to attend group from 6:00-9:00 p.m. each day. I don't remember the specifics of my jar ceremony, but I do remember Vanessa telling me that I strongly positively influenced the entire group, and that I should use my powers for good.

I thought, powers? What am I, like a junkie superhero? Initially, I found it laughable, but it's interesting the way others can see things in you that you can't see in yourself. She was right. I recognized that I had a lot of influence on the 20 or so people that were in there with me. Not in an ego-maniacal way or anything like that but being the seasoned rehab veteran with a large majority of folks at their first treatment, I think a lot of them took their cue from me.

On my very last evening in PHP, I was bullshitting with my roommate and Blaze. Dan came in with the orange 'Rob 37 Heroin' cake that you see adorning the cover of this book. I lost it! It was fucking hilarious! Soon after, Maurice, one of the technicians, came in to do his 15-30 minute room check. I made him snap that picture and text it to me on my cell phone which I would get back the following day when I slid over to IOP. Everyone had been referring to me as 'rob 37 heroin' going back to Gateway West, but that truly solidified it. I had die-cut stickers of it made and handed them out to my friends. If you look hard enough around downtown Naperville and Aurora at dumpsters, ashtrays, etc., you might be lucky enough to spot one of them still there.

The first day back out after two months was incredibly freeing. I wasn't exactly flushed for cash, so I had to be frugal, but I did enjoy exploring NaperThrill—wandering around, snapping photos, and just taking things in. After a couple of days, I began posting up at the Nichols Library, cleaned up my resume, and began looking for a job. I made it a regular thing to hit up the 3:00 p.m. meeting at the West Suburban Fellowship Club (WSFC). This schedule allowed me enough time to look for work in the morning, head to the meeting, and still make it back to housing in time to catch the van ride over to clinical for evening group at 6:00 p.m.

After a week of this routine, I was outside of the WSFC chiefing a Newport before the meeting when my former boss called me.

"Hey man, how are you doing?"
"I'm doing pretty good."
"So, what have you been up to?"

I thought, looking for a fucking job mutherfucker! Or did you already forget you fired me a few weeks ago which nearly sent me on a downward spiral into oblivion? But instead, I said, "About to hit up an AA meeting, looking for a job man."

"Whoa, whoa, pump the brakes. Hey man, I need you brother. This company needs you, but I need to know you're doing okay, putting your recovery first and that you're able to handle it."
"Okay."

"Yeah, you jacked up everybody's health insurance premiums with all your "vacations," but if you want, I'm willing to bring you back as a 1099 employee [a contractor]. Would you be interested?"

"Yeah, maybe I could work half days or something from home [i.e., rehab housing] like I did before, for the next month or two until I completed IOP, and then we can go from there," I said.

"Alright cool, let me work out the logistics and how to proceed and we can get you rocking and rolling next week."

I hung up and I was ecstatic. Sure, I had to put my pride aside a bit, but I was working a program and grateful to have a job again after several awkward phone interviews. Things continued to work out. I kept doing the next right thing.

The following week, I worked half days from housing, headed to the 3:00 p.m. meeting, and then to group in the evening. I was living with Adam, Jacob, and Kodi, all of whom worked together in downtown NaperThrill at Le Chocolate. It seemed like things were falling into place and although I had a job, I wasn't going to be getting a decent size paycheck for at least a few weeks. I was completely preoccupied with what to do when my insurance ran out and I had to find somewhere to stay.

Around this same time, my sex drive was coming back with a vengeance. I had been married to the needle for over eight years and now I was thirsty as fuck. I downloaded and set up profiles on eight or nine dating apps on my phone. I even went so far as to get set up on Fetish and S&M sites—shit was crazy man.

I kept plugging along, fueled by caffeine and nicotine, and things were working well. On November 21, my IOP counselor Donnie, told me that my insurance would only pay for eight more days of IOP. I thought I had another five weeks. Fuck. I had hardly any money and there was no way I was going to have enough saved up to move anywhere. I had entrenched myself in the recovery scene of Naperville between Banyan and the WSFC, and I wanted to stay in the area.

My only other option was to head to a halfway house in Joliet, which was willing to take me in on good faith for a couple of weeks before I got paid and could start paying rent. But I knew that if I landed in Joliet there would be no way to make it back to Naperville.

I would have to start from scratch and find my way again, meet new people, find meetings I liked, etc. It wasn't desirable, so I began scouring Craigslist and apartment rental sites. I asked Brad, the head of housing operations, if I could stay for an extra day or two until I got paid on the first of the month. He was able to help me out, but I was scrambling.

I checked out a few places, but most wanted a one-month security deposit, and I didn't like any of them. In addition, they were inconvenient for someone who didn't have a vehicle. When I had one day remaining at housing, I was convinced that the half-way house in Joliet was my future. I had one last place to check out in Warrenville. It was a Taiwanese woman and her three-year-old son. She had an extra bedroom in their townhome available to rent month-to-month for $500. I checked it out and it was great.

"I like it, I wanna move in. What do I have to do?" I asked.

"Well let me talk it over with my husband who's working out in California, and I will text you later."

"Yeah, I have to be out of my current space by the first of the month so the sooner the better."

"Okay cool," she said.

"Do you have any questions for me anything?" I asked.

She straight-up said, "You're not like a drug addict or anything, right?"

"Of course not."

Later that afternoon I got the text, and everything seemed to be falling into place. It was this pattern of things working out for me, unlike anything I had ever experienced before in my entire life. If I just kept doing the right things, at the right time, for the right reasons, then I kept getting the right results.

You know, I often ask people how they found "hope" in their recovery, and I get a wide variety of answers, all over the spectrum. For me, this is when I started garnering hope and buying into the whole recovery thing and the principles of the program. I was building momentum and it seemed like all the little things I was doing each day were adding up to successes. Life was becoming manageable for me for the first time. I couldn't remember ever having the sense of calmness and serenity that I had during this period. It's like the A.A. Promises describe, I intuitively knew how to handle situations that used to baffle me. I moved in a day later and it seemed like nothing could knock me off course. I quickly settled into my new routine. Working from the townhouse. Heading to a meeting most days. Sliding into Le Chocolate where several of my former roommates and buddies from rehab now worked, and then eventually made my way back home with a weekly outpatient visit to Banyan mixed in.

A few days later, Christmas was coming up. Tyler called and said, "Hey bro, Adam's dead man, he OD'd."
"Really?"

"Yeah man, they found him at a hotel."
"Shitty."

I have had friends die in my bedroom and have known several others that overdosed or took their own lives, but I had been roommates with Adam up until three weeks ago. I had spent a month with him 24-7 in rehab. The memories were fresh. I didn't cry or break down or lose my shit, but something changed. Something shifted. His death lit a fire under my ass and taught me to turn that pain into purpose.

His family held a memorial for him at Le Chocolate a few days later and I met several of his family members and loved ones. It was a relatively upbeat celebration of life, but you could see the pain behind their eyes. They had unanswered questions about Adam. I think they were hoping to garner some answers from those of us who had been living with him for the past couple of months. It was such a powerful experience, and I feel grateful for having had the opportunity to know him. It solidified the connection between the six or seven of us who are still sober today. Although unfortunate, it may have been the catalyst for our successful recoveries and truly the tie that binds.

A month later we reconvened to spread some of his ashes along the Riverwalk in Naperville. We marched to a serene spot. Jacob threw on *Atlantic City* by The Band, a somewhat hidden gem, and one of Adam's favorite songs. It was like an eerie trumpet call over a lost battlefield. Gratitude. A reminder to keep working and help anyone who might be out there suffering.

# 10

# Conclusion

As I write this, it's Labor Day 2021 and in a couple of days, on September 8th, I'll be celebrating four years of sobriety. As I reflect on my journey, and reread some of the stories contained herein, it's wild to think about where I am today. I'm one of the lucky ones. Sure, it took dozens of rehabs and treatment centers and was by no means a linear process, but I made it. In the past four years, I've learned a lot, changed a lot, and I've lost friends along the way; friends who didn't want to change with me.

Never in my wildest dreams did I envision the life I have today, and I mean that in the best possible way. When I entered my recovery journey back in 1999, and even at the start of this most recent adventure back in September 2017, you couldn't have told me I'd ever enjoy doing service work, volunteering, and helping others. Sure, I'd heard through the years things like, "we can only keep what we have by giving it away," and that we need to be "of maximum service to others." My response was always, fuck that man. If I can just figure out how to stop doing heroin it would be a win. If there was any way possible to find enjoyment without drugs and alcohol, then that would be a cherry on top. The ideas escaped me for the longest time; maybe I just wasn't ready to hear it until I finally was ready to hear it. Until I hit rock bottom.

Drugs and alcohol were not my problem, they were my solution. Every time I needed to escape, or felt uncomfortable, I reached for what I knew would quickly and efficiently put me back at ease. On the other hand, if I was feeling good, I knew drugs would make me feel even better. When I was clean back in 2012, I learned that simply abstaining from drugs and alcohol was miserable. I thought that my life would improve if I just didn't use. But it didn't. I was still a hot mess. I had fleeting moments of what I'll call okay-ed-ness, but it wasn't sustainable.

A buddy of mine described it this way, "It's like taking the transmission out of a car. If you do that it won't run right, and you need to replace it with a new one for the car to function."

That's how it was for me. Without strategy, change is just a substitution. You could take the drugs and alcohol out of my life, but I needed to replace them with something to restore the balance. I needed to fill the void that was left by my best friend – heroin.

At first, it was hard. I had to start getting comfortable being uncomfortable. That's what early sobriety is. It's uncomfortable. Those feelings you drowned out with booze and drugs come to the surface and you start to feel "better." And by that, I mean you feel every emotion better, the good ones and the bad ones. You feel emotions "more" when you're not completely numbed out by substances.

I had to remain open-minded and willing to try new things. Early on, I adopted the serenity prayer as my go-to mantra when things got tough. To this day, I still use that as the lens to view every new situation. I put every situation through that lens, particularly when I feel stuck. I ask, is this something I need to accept, or is it something I can change? If it's something I need to accept, I try not to obsess over it and waste mental equity worrying about it. I keep moving. It can be easier said than done, but be patient with your improvement.

Over time I've gotten much better at letting go. I describe trying to muscle through a situation that I should accept like trying to drive a car with your elbows. When I try to control things, it ends up being very difficult and I struggle, I can't turn or pivot easily, but once I let go and stop trying to fix, manage and control everything it's so much easier. When I take my hands off the wheel and let things happen naturally, it's like I'm in a self-driving Tesla and everything goes smoothly. It's a relief to let go of control and situations don't drain me emotionally and physically.

By nature, I'm introverted and keep to myself. Normally, I don't initiate a lot of conversations, particularly with people I don't know very well. It was uncomfortable once I left treatment and had to continue my recovery journey without my buddies from treatment. It was easy to sit in meetings or go to the store with more than a dozen or so other guys that I knew well but once I was discharged and left to my own devices, it was different. I missed being at housing and surrounded by other people in early recovery.

As I mentioned, I had heard that the opposite of addiction is connection and as challenging as that could be for me, I made it a top priority to stay connected to the recovery community, to the people I met in treatment, and other people who were trying to improve their lives. I started getting outside of myself and getting involved. I was doing the things I had always refused to do.

I got a sponsor. I worked the steps. I went to different types of meetings and explored different types of recovery programs. I got the booty juice, the Vivitrol shot, something I'd never been willing to do before. It was like I was taking out every possible insurance policy I could to prevent slipping and going back out. I started to see my life getting dramatically better by following the suggestions that I'd heard from folks for almost two decades. Doing the right things, at the right times, for the right reasons kept giving me the right results. I remained teachable and open-minded and willing. I started to gather momentum.

After a while, things became astronomically better than they were on September 7, 2017. If my situation was only slightly better than it was back then, I wouldn't still be doing this shit. I'd probably be dead or high right now. If following this path wasn't a total blast and I wasn't having fun every day, I wouldn't be doing it.

For 18 years, I doubted everyone who said these things and every book I read about recovery, thinking they were trying to sell me their solution and it wasn't mine. Now I'm the guy saying it. I'm okay with that. In the four-plus years I've been sober, I've met some of the most amazing and inspiring individuals. I found a sense of community. The void I'd spent decades trying to fill with dope is now full of human connections. I found a place where I fit in for the first time in my life and I've been blessed with amazing opportunities to grow and help others.

I hope you can learn from my experience and avoid making the same mistakes I did. Seek out people who truly care about you and let go of people who don't. Listen to the people who want to help you. Try every treatment option available. Open yourself up and connect with others. It's hard work but if I can do it, so can you.

There are too many people to thank everyone, but you know who you are, and I can't do this alone. YOU make it worth it for me every day. That's why I keep coming back.

## One Last Thing...

Now, you may have noticed a 15yr gap from 1999-to-2014 that was missing from this collection. I was advised by editors and publishers to trim my page count, but a lot of heavy shit went down during that time. Multiple suicide attempts, getting engaged to a Ugandan during a drunken blackout, arrests, jail time, being held up at gunpoint, friends dying in my apartment, etc.

Stay tuned for Volume II. If this collection of miscellaneous stories is kind of about how it started and how it ended, the second collection will go into detail about the agony of fifteen years of drug-filled chaos. The *in-between* years if you will.

Thank you so much for spending some time and joining me for a walk down memory (or nightmare) lane and regardless of what you thought about the book, I would be incredibly grateful for you to throw a review up on Amazon.

Thank you!